THE ALASKAN BLONDE

BLONDE

Sex, Secrets and the Hollywood Story that Shocked America

THE ALASKAN BLONDE

Sex, Secrets and the Hollywood
Story that Shocked America

James T. Bartlett

Territory Books

ISBN 978-0-9849730-2-6

Acknowledgements

This book would not have happened without the endless help of these archivists, librarians, and historians: Leah Geibel and Abby Focht at Alaska State Archives, Claire Imamura at Alaska State Library, Arabeth Balasko at Anchorage Museum, Becky Butler at University of Alaska Fairbanks & Anchorage, Fawn Carter at Rasmuson Library University of Alaska Fairbanks, Mike Maddox at Klein Texas Family History Center, Puget Sound Regional Archives, Noel Wien Public Library in Fairbanks, Harris County Clerk's Office in Texas, Michael Holland at Los Angeles City Archives, Edward Winter at Los Angeles County Medical Examiner-Coroner, Washington State Patrol, Helen Ofield at Lemon Grove Historical Society, Fairbanks Genealogy Society, Tanana-Yukon Historical Society, the "You're Probably From Fairbanks If You Can Remember" and "Alaska History & You" Facebook Groups, Michael Stroup at Maria Kip Orphanage, Taylor Ostman at Dignity Memorial, Diana Pfeiffer at Alaska Sales & Service, and Theodore Hovey at Hollywood Forever Cemetery.

Adele Virgin, Patty Wagner Messer, Michael Carey, Stella Carpenter, Colleen Redman, Donald V. Smiley, Sally Murphy and Deverick Martin helped me with interviews and research, while Catherine Pelonero, Kim Stout, Rochelle Staab and Tammy Kaehler read my drafts and gave me invaluable advice. Susan McCall helped with the infuriating task of formatting, and despite my endless changes, Nina Monet did a fantastic job, once again, with the cover art.

Thanks also to Kory Eberhardt at A Taste of Alaska Lodge, everyone at The Big I and the Mecca, and the teams at Explore Fairbanks, Visit Houston, Visit Conroe and Visit Sugar Land.

Photo Credits: Darrell Rafferty, Saundra Kinnaird, Cecelia Richard, Patty Wagner Messer, John Warren, AP Photos, Wendall Thomas, James T. Bartlett.

And may the following people rest in peace: Candy Waugaman, Byron Halvorson, Terrence Cole, Peter Parkin, Grady Thomas, Genie Buscarini and Judy Morris (née Martin).

Dedication

This book is for the children, grandchildren, great-grandchildren, and friends of Cecil, Diane, Johnny Warren, and William Colombany. Even if it might be difficult to read at times, I really hope it brings them some clarity, and maybe even some closure.

The Alaskan Blonde would not have happened without the endless support and encouragement of my wife, Wendall Thomas, who strongly felt that this was a story that needed to be told, and insisted that I keep writing. This book is dedicated to her.

Contents

Acknowledgements..*v*

Dedication...*vii*

Introduction..*xi*

Main Characters..*xvii*

Chapter 1 – Breaking the Law for Love.................................1

Chapter 2 – Far North..7

Chapter 3 – "It's too late for Cecil"....................................14

Chapter 4 – Witness Statements 19

Chapter 5 – "Shut up, or I will kill you".............................25

Chapter 6 – The Autopsy...32

Chapter 7 – The Forensics...37

Chapter 8 – The Photographs..43

Chapter 9 – Inquest No. 285...47

Chapter 10 – Johnny Talks...57

Chapter 11 – Arrested for Murder 62

Chapter 12 – Diana/Diane 68

Chapter 13 – Broken Sweethearts 71

Chapter 14 – Texas..80

Chapter 15 – My Only Father 87

Chapter 16 – "Plain and simple case of murder" 95

Chapter 17 – The Unpublished Memoir............................110

Chapter 18 – Bloody Pajamas..118

Chapter 19 – Pulp Star..125

Chapter 20 – Barbara/Doris..128

Chapter 21 – A Scarlet Letter..136

Chapter 22 – Millionaire Orphan...145

Chapter 23 – Searching for Marquam 152

Chapter 24 – An Uncomfortable Reminder.........................158

Chapter 25 – Another Home Invasion 163

Chapter 26 – The Third Suspect 169

Chapter 27 – Filet mignon in L.A. 173

Chapter 28 – Exonerated..180

Chapter 29 – Intruders...189

Chapter 30 – Professional Hit? 195

Chapter 31 – Mr. X the White Knight 201

Chapter 32 – The Alaskan Blonde 208

Chapter 33 – October 17, 1953 213

Epilogue...*217*

Bibliography...*221*

About The Author *229*

Introduction

"…remains to this day the most notorious and baffling murder in the history of Fairbanks."
Terrence Cole, Fairbanks historian and author of
Fighting for the Forty-Ninth Star

The digital clock beside my bed was inching towards 2am, and it was almost exactly 65 years since the murder.

I was looking out the hotel window at the damp streets of Fairbanks, Alaska, watching late-night drinkers stumbling along 2nd Avenue. The first snows of winter were overdue, and I had been warned that the temperatures might dip as low as minus 30.

The cars parked on the street below had cables poking out from under car hoods (something that puzzled me when I arrived). I learned that once connected to the electricity they keep the engine from freezing, while the colorful flags on the hydrants make it easy for firefighters to locate them when they get buried in snow — and to stop you crashing your car into them.

A short distance behind 2nd Avenue was the Northward Building, one of the tallest structures in downtown. Its distinctive "H" shape and utilitarian, corrugated-clad design still make it stand out, even if it's fallen a long way from its golden era as the swankiest residence in town — when, in October 1953, it was the location of the first Alaskan murder to make headlines in America, and around the world.

In the 1950s the murder rate in America was around 5.1% per 100,000 people, and though figures for then-territorial Alaska were limited (and all statistics have varying factors), after gaining statehood in 1959 it placed 10th in the list of murder rates, with 7.8% per 100,000 people. The numbers among "non-whites" were shockingly higher, a wide gap that sadly still remains today.

However, despite a long-standing reputation for violent crime, murders in Alaska rarely made the news in what many call the "Outside" or the "Lower 48". While Alaska was still a territory, only a couple of larger stories from territorial times broke through to be covered by the major newspapers.

The first had a Fairbanks connection and happened in 1912, though it didn't hit the wires until 1934, when a 51-year-old sailor was arrested for drunkenness in New York. His appearance reminded veteran officers of a triple murderer nicknamed the "Blueberry Kid", and fingerprints seemed to confirm a match.

Allegedly, "Blueberry Kid" Tommy Johnson had been hired by prospector "Fiddler John" Holmberg, his likely wife, Fairbanks prostitute "Dutch Marie" Schmidt, and "Tamarack" Frank Adams to take them up the Koyukuk tributary to meet a Yukon River steamboat. The next time Johnson was seen in Seattle he was alone, and had a pouch of some $8,000 in gold dust and nuggets (around $208,000 today). He allegedly sold a bracelet that belonged to Marie, too.

In 1914 hers was the first — and only — body to be found, which bought Fairbanks law enforcement into the investigation, but to no avail. Later in 1934, the hapless sailor was set free: he had a glass eye, a distinguishing feature that would not have been missed in 1912. Johnson was never caught, and in 1938 the indictment was dismissed for lack of evidence.

In 1917 an Associated Press wire reported that Edward Krause, the "Alaskan Pirate" who had escaped from death row in Juneau, had been shot by a shopkeeper. Krause was suspected of five murders between 1913 and 1915, though there was only enough evidence to connect him to one of the victims. Both Krause and Johnson were suspected of further killings.

This 1953 murder was very different. It was a scandalous domestic murder for a start, and it had even more lurid, irresistible ingredients. The case drew photographers and reporters from newspapers in Seattle, Oakland and San Francisco, while many others took coverage from the news agencies. The killing also made the pages of *Life*, *Newsweek*, *Jet*, a number of pulp magazines, and the pages of the *Los Angeles Times*, which is where I first read about it.

After moving to L.A. in 2004 I had struggled to adapt to the sheer size of the city, and I couldn't find a guide that told me as much about the history (both good and bad, especially the bad), of the bar or restaurant I might be drinking in.

In 2012 I published an alternative guide called *Gourmet Ghosts — Los Angeles*, but it was when I was researching *Gourmet Ghosts 2* that I came across a story about an unhappy-looking blonde who had checked into a Hollywood hotel, and was linked to the scandalous murder of Cecil Wells in far-off Alaska.

I was intrigued — then amazed — to find there was no book, movie or radio drama about it, and I couldn't find many contemporary references to it either, save for a review of a show in which actors in period costume played famous and infamous people, and "Cecil Wells" told his story while standing next to "his" gravestone.

Aside from a little over eight pages in the invaluable *Fighting for the Forty-Ninth Star*, the case got short shrift, if it was mentioned at all, in general books about Alaska and Fairbanks. There was also nothing hiding on the shelves in the Noel Wien Public Library in Fairbanks, nor in the University of Alaska Fairbanks collections.

Even so, there was no big moment when I decided to begin *The Alaskan Blonde*, let alone when I decided on that title, but I first started writing about it in my journal in late 2016, and an entry from February 4, 2017 reads: "It's great — wild, outrageous, confusing, overwhelming."

I had also quickly realized that, ominously, it was a very, very cold case. All the people involved at the time were long dead, so unlike *Fatal Vision* by Joe McGinnis or *The Stranger Beside Me* by Ann Rule, I knew from the start that I could not have a direct, personal connection to the people involved. There were no surviving victims, no killer languishing away in prison, and no adults left who were there at the time –or so I thought.

The closest I would be able to get would be children or grandchildren — if they agreed to talk to me. My journalistic background helped, as I was used to keeping a distance and sticking to the facts, but even then some family members just didn't want to talk. Several were very wary of me, at least initially: I was a stranger, and they couldn't understand why I was interested in a story from so long ago.

The further I got into my research and the more interviews I carried out, the more I was certain that I really wanted to know what happened — for the sake of those family members at least. Maybe there had been a cover-up, or a conspiracy of silence, or what happened was an open family secret?

I also found that there was a unique political angle to the case: Alaska's fight to obtain statehood.

I was surprised to learn that it had been a controversial, complicated and decades-long campaign, and that despite the booms associated with gold, furs, fish or natural resources, it had always seemed a distant dream tangled up in red tape. Ruled from afar and with no real representation, it was easy to see how a resentment built up among the citizens. How could the politicians in Washington, D.C. know what it was like living in Nome, or Anchorage, or Barrow, let alone what those inhabitants might need in their vast homeland?

Alternatively, many in the corridors of power over 4,000 miles away looked at the huge landmass, the small population (in 1950 a quarter of Alaska's 128,000 people were in Anchorage, with the 19,000 or so of Fairbanks a distant second), and saw it as an endless financial drain — until WWII began.

The massive federal spend during and beyond the war years made statehood inevitable, but becoming that 49th star on Saturday, January 3, 1959 is still very much recent history for all Alaskans. Even so, many residents still consider themselves separate, even from the capital Juneau, which is a southern geographic panhandle more Canada-adjacent than Alaska "proper."

Victim Cecil Wells was staunchly pro-statehood, and even appeared on national radio's "America's Town Meeting of the Air" debate program about the subject, but several disappointed — and even angry — members of his family told me that not only had Cecil's murder been forgotten, they felt it had been swept under the carpet as Alaska focused on the big prize.

Even before that, way back in 1878, the only federal official in Alaska said "the frozen truth" was that Alaskans had no rights at all:

"A man may get murdered in Alaska, his will forged, and his estate scattered to the four corners of the earth, and there is no power in a court of chancery to redress it."

Just over a century later Everett Hepp, a former superior court judge, made a similar observation: "It was said that to kill a moose was a greater offense than to kill a person."

In a different way, the question of statehood often affected my research. Territorial archives and records were often missing or incomplete, while post-statehood ones were usually accurate and easily available. Of course, it was Murphy's Law that this murder happened well before statehood, but this was just another challenging twist in what was beginning to seem like the ultimate noir — and I was hooked.

More than that, I was struck by the fact that though the murder happened in a time of rigid social rules, our supposedly more enlightened times really wouldn't change how this would be served up for consumption today. The murder, money, sex and race would still get the same reactions and judgments from the media and the public.

How Diane Wells, Cecil's wife, was described in the press — sweet-voiced, curvaceous, slim, blue eyed, pretty, willowy, comely, a woman in a million, a blonde temptress, and the highly-dubious "playgirl" — all seemed familiar in today's Instagram age, even with the growing influence of #timesup.

As for African-American Johnny Warren, he was solely described as a "negro", (though the occasional addition of the term "boy" was especially racist in its overtones). When I first read about his involvement in the case I was sure that he was going to be punished, even if he didn't pull the trigger. Again, even though this had happened in the fiery times of Jim Crow America, I felt that things would still go the same way today.

Back in 1953 it would have been impossible for Diane to reveal her true feelings, and while the truth about what happened was more complicated than sex, it wouldn't be fully uncovered until nearly 70 years later.

Main Characters

Cecil Wells — murdered on October 17, 1953

Ethel — Cecil's fourth wife

Phyllis, Cecil Jr, Wendell — children from Cecil's previous marriages

Darrell Rafferty & Cathi McMurrin — Cecil's grandchildren

Diane Wells — Cecil's fifth wife, charged with his first-degree murder

Florence Hill (later known as Yvonne) — Diane's mother

Donald Henry Walker — Diane's first husband

Saundra & Bonnie — Diane & Donald's children

Marquam Wells — Cecil and Diane's son; aged three when he inherited the family estate

Marq Wells — Marquam's son, born December 1967

Johnny C. Warren — Diane's alleged lover; also charged with first-degree murder

Ladell Willia — Johnny's sister

Clara — Johnny's third wife

John Charles — son of Johnny and his fifth wife Ellen

William Barillas Colombany — "The Third Suspect"

Norma Fullon (née Colombany) — Colombany's granddaughter

Robert Caffee — witness in Colombany's 1955 trial

Investigators

Theodore "Ted" Stevens — Fairbanks District Attorney

E.V. Danforth — Fairbanks Chief of Police

Frank Wirth — US Deputy Marshal, Fairbanks

Al Dorsh, Jr — US Marshal, Fairbanks

Clyde Dailey & Wendell H. Paust — Seattle Police detectives hired by the Wells Family

Others

Judy Morris — Ethel's half-sister, and companion to Diane when she first arrived in Fairbanks

Juida Gail — friend of Diane and Colombany

Lloyd & Sally Martin — business partner/friends of Cecil and Diane

Reuben & Clara Tarte — friends of Cecil and Diane

CHAPTER 1

Breaking the Law for Love

Today, Cecil and Diane Wells would be called a power couple. They were certainly more A-List than B-List, but the pulp magazines really spiced them up anyway.

Front Page Detective wrote that Cecil was "was no longer so lithe on the dance floor, but still had one of the most flexible bank rolls in Fairbanks and carried more weight than a Japanese wrestler," while Diane "was estimated by most of the virile men in town, with hair the color of honey, and the shapeliest legs this side of a chorus line… she lived a life of mink coats, diamond brooches and gold bracelets."

Though his dark hair was just starting to recede, Cecil Moore Wells was still a handsome, smartly-dressed, 50 year old businessman with four ex-wives, five children, and interests in the automobile industry, real estate, oil and mining. He always drove the latest two door Cadillac Eldorado, had just been elected president of the All Alaska Chamber of Commerce, and was a $10,000 "booster" for the flag-waving Fairbanks Community Hotel project.

His life had been that of a pioneer; at a young age he traveled cross country with his family in a Model T Ford, speculated for gold — and spent 13 months in federal prison for love.

This wasn't a secret, and locating the court records and a copy of his signature when he was admitted as convict number 3894 on May 1, 1928 was straightforward. His crime seems almost absurd today, but back then it was very serious.

A complaint had been filed against Cecil and Maud Raudabaugh for "Cohabitation in a state of adultery. Since December 1927 to February 1928,

1

they had "feloniously, willfully and unlawfully... continuously cohabiting and live with each other in a state of adultery... in a public place."

Maud and Cecil were however married to other people, and so were in violation of Section 2001 of the *Compiled Laws of the Territory of Alaska*, an offense that carried a two-year sentence and/or a $500 fine. They had in fact been living together for longer than that, and so pleaded guilty. Cecil was sentenced to 13 months at McNeil Island, out in Puget Sound, Washington state, while Maud was fined $400 plus costs (about $4,000 today).

McNeil was no holiday camp with razor wire. At various times it also played host to Charles Manson, gangster Mickey Cohen, and Robert Franklin Stroud.

A psychopathic pimp, Stroud was convicted of manslaughter in Juneau in 1909, and gave his first impression of McNeil in *Distant Justice: Policing the Alaska Frontier*:

"The stench was that of dead, cold air, the old odor of unwashed bodies, unsanitary night buckets, the accumulated filth of years."

Stroud killed a guard while in Leavenworth Prison in Kansas in 1916, but newspaper readers in the Lower 48 didn't really know his name until the 1960s, when he was dubbed the "Birdman of Alcatraz", and was the subject of a movie adaptation starring Burt Lancaster.

Unlike Stroud, who was notoriously violent to both staff and his fellow inmates, Cecil served his time quietly and without incident, and was released early on February 24, 1929, with time off for good behavior.

By then he had divorced his first wife Elmina, and he married Maud right after his release from prison. He went from success to success in Anchorage, opening Wells Garage in 1930 with an innovative scheme. At the time customers in Alaska selected cars from a catalog before they were shipped to them, but Cecil decided to bring a number of cars for use as showroom models, and to offer the possibility of test drives.

In the following years he added several more automobiles to his distribution roster, dealt with tractors and mining equipment, and started a local bus line and taxi service. In 1939 after he and Maud divorced, Cecil and his third wife Nanele and their son, Cecil Junior, moved to Fairbanks. There he opened the

Wells Alaska Motor Company, which some older Fairbanksians still remember, though now it's the location of the Rabinowitz Courthouse.

He sold his Anchorage operation, which still exists today under the name Alaska Sales & Service, and also invested in Chena Hot Springs, one of Fairbanks' most famous tourist attractions, and in a major $1,350,000 Hawaiian condominium project alongside friend Lloyd Martin. The 12 storey Roselei Apartments building was completed after Cecil's death.

His fourth marriage was to Ethel Hedges, a local store owner, in 1941. They had a son, Wendell, born in 1943 and apparently named after Wendell Avenue, a long road that ran alongside Cecil's car dealership, though that marriage also ended in divorce. He may not have had much luck with matrimony, but Cecil was a man of influence, and this meant he often met notable people who passed through Fairbanks — including one of the most famous people in the world: Walt Disney.

One of his grandchildren, Darrell Rafferty, explained that Walt and his daughter Sharon had visited Alaska in the 1940s, and Cecil was asked to help show them around. While they were there, the story went, Walt and Sharon fed ground squirrels, and this inspired the creation of Chip n' Dale, the squeaky-voiced, mischievous chipmunks.

Newspaper reports confirmed that Disney and Sharon had gone to Alaska in August 1947. They were among a group of passengers on a plane piloted by Russ Havenstrite, the head of an oil field development near Anchorage, and visited there along with stops in Juneau, Fairbanks, and Candle, a former gold mine that Darrell said was home to the ground squirrels.

Havenstrite was partners with Disney, producer Darryl F. Zanuck (*The Grapes of Wrath*, *All About Eve*), comedy producer Hal Roach (Laurel & Hardy's *The Music Box*), and businessman Carlton Beal in the oil venture, though Disney was also on a research mission, as soon afterward he commissioned the first in the Oscar-winning series of "True-Life Adventure" movies.

The Walt Disney Family Museum website features a 1956 interview Diane and Sharon Disney gave to the *Saturday Evening Post* when they talked about the trip, but Darrell had real proof: snapshots of Cecil and Walt together.

One showed Walt, with his trademark mustache, a camera around his neck, and what seems to be a light meter in his hand, talking face-to-face with Cecil. There is a second, blurrier shot that seemed to be Disney kneeling down, and ones of Sharon panning for gold, as she said she had done in the *Post* interview, and of her with a ground squirrel.

Comparing those snapshots to the website post showed Sharon with the same pigtails and red boots, while Walt had the same camera and hat. There were two snapshots of Cecil feeding ground squirrels as well, but as charming as they might have been, those furry critters weren't the inspiration for Chip n' Dale: they had first appeared back in 1943.

It was surely a great story to tell Diane, who Cecil met in a bar in Seattle a year or so later.

Theirs seemed to be a whirlwind romance, and Darrell said that Cecil "pretty much married her on the spot," he said. "He didn't know her for very long, but he didn't really care. He was just interested in a trophy wife."

That may have been the case, and Cecil's romantic feelings made him brush up against the law once again.

Diane, 20 years younger than Cecil, was very different from his previous wives. The camera loved her striking blonde looks, and she really stood out in a crowd; even more so in Fairbanks. A long-time resident described her as a lovely lady who, despite being "high society, honey," was always very friendly:

"She didn't walk around with her nose in the air."

In interviews, both men and women commented on Diane's beauty.

"There was nobody that was more beautiful than that girl. She was just knockout beautiful," said one woman, while another man recalled that "She was good lookin', slim, everything was a plus on her. I can understand why Cecil picked her out from the herd. He always had an eye for the pretty ones."

Cecil and Diane were married in Fairbanks on September 25, 1949, and it was true that Diane was always well-dressed, with jewelry often a feature, and her curly blonde hair always fashionably styled.

Family members agreed that Cecil was happy she made him look good, but in a city populated by so many young, single men, he must have had some moments of jealousy.

Whether that was true or not, marriage saw Diane becoming stepmother to Cecil's five other children, three of whom were almost her age. Like most women of the era she spent most of her time running the home and looking after their own son Marquam, who was born in August 1950, and known to be rather boisterous.

Cecil Wells Junior mentioned there were "issues" with Marquam, but that he felt Diane was attentive and maternal to her young son, and was a good stepmother too. He also recalled when he visited Fairbanks one summer:

"Diane and I laughed a lot. It was kind of funny because she was 30 years old at the time, but she always introduced me as her son. People would look at her askance and say, 'How old were you when you had him?' (He was 15), but she never bothered to add the adjective 'stepson'."

He also remembered when she stuck up for him:

"The day I left Fairbanks my father was entertaining some important military people, and it was time for me to go to the airport to get on my plane. Diane took me into the living room and she said, 'Cecil Junior is leaving.' My dad looked and said, 'Well I suppose he needs some money.' Diane said, 'No, he's been working all the time he's been here.' I worked for my dad in the garage, (and she said) 'He's been working and he's saved all that money'."

Cecil Junior felt that Diane treated him as a contemporary, or at least in an adult way, though he did recall an awkward moment:

"She gave me hell one time. She was walking back from town to the house, and I pulled up in a car next to her, and she gave me hell because of course there was no pavement there. She had just washed her hair, and the dust got all through it."

One interviewee joked that "pretty much every man in town had a crush on Diane," and Darrell said that "(Cecil) photographed her constantly. He was quite sold on her. I don't think there was much more to it than that."

Darrell sent me a number of travel snapshots of Cecil and Diane, who had visited Brazil, Mexico, Peru, Chile, Guatemala, the West Indies and Hawaii together, ones of Diane with a candled cake, in a flower-filled hothouse, and several other memorable moments. Cecil's Chamber of Commerce roles meant extensive travel, and he often flew to them in his Cessna airplane; he and Diane regularly also featured in the "Social" section of the local newspaper.

There were many smiles in the snapshots, and they seemed to be a happy couple enjoying the luxury of international travel at a time when it wasn't available to everyone. Being in color rather than black and white newsprint really made them seem real too, and put everything into focus. However, when I looked at the pictures, I couldn't help but wonder: how long was this before the murder?

CHAPTER 2

Far North

Despite already having a family connection to Fairbanks (an uncle of hers had been mayor back in the 1920s), the new Mrs. Wells still needed a way to break the conversational ice. Moving there would have been quite an adjustment, at least compared to her time living in metropolitan cities like Portland, San Francisco and Seattle, and she was later quoted as saying that it was "boring" in Fairbanks.

Known as the "Golden Heart" of Alaska, it was a conservative, church-going city. The 1950 census, which the Wells family would have been included in, listed the city population as just 5,771, with almost three times that in the surrounding area — not including the military. In a 1982 interview, former Fairbanks superior court judge Everett Hepp recalled the city as being "rough and ready," and to many it seemed like a kind of polar Wild West, in part because of the male-dominated population.

Like Florida and California, Alaska was (and still is) a place where you can go to start over. Alaska is bigger than Texas, California and Montana combined at close to 664,000 square miles, so it's easy to get lost and stay lost, especially if you avoid Anchorage (which has always been by far the biggest city, and is currently home to over a third of the state's population). In the days before computers, credit cards and cell phones it was even easier: you could go almost anywhere and get a new name or family, complete with legal paperwork, and have a good chance of never being exposed.

Alaska has gone through several boom-bust cycles too, and I learned that there's opposition and even resentment towards the many transitory people who come to town to make their fortune, but don't interact with the

7

community. Not only does this reinforce a sense of separatism, but the terms "greenhorn," "tenderfoot," and even the Native term *Cheechako* (or "newcomer") still get used, especially by "Sourdoughs," the nickname for old-timers who have lived here for decades.

It's not easy for new arrivals anywhere though, which is probably why Cecil asked Judy Morris to be a friendly face to welcome Diane, and help her settle into Cecil's home on Illinois Street.

Born and raised in and around Los Angeles, Judy had found Fairbanks a culture shock when she moved there a few years before — also at Cecil's request. Judy was the half-sister of Cecil's then-wife Ethel, and since he was away on business so frequently, he felt Ethel needed help not only looking after their son Wendell, but also dealing with his extended family, several of whom were also living in the home.

Now aged 96, Judy recalled that she was happy to help, but the initial sibling obligation to go North wasn't exactly appealing to a young, single woman:

"It was like landing on another planet, and I told my mother I would be back in 30 days!" she laughed, noting that in fact she fell in love with Fairbanks, and ended up staying for 70 years.

Judy was married and had a son by the time she met Diane, and the relationship between the two was more care-giving and domestic, rather than social. "I was just there to talk to her," she says, admitting that Diane was "nice to be around," and that while they did become friends, they didn't talk or meet much after Marquam was born — or at least not without their respective husbands. There was another reason for Cecil wanting Judy's help too: Diane was several months pregnant.

Additionally, it was early 1950, and in Fairbanks much of the population, especially outside the main area, were still living in wooden shacks that were colorful, smart and cozy, but might have seemed very rural to visitors — even dirty and unwelcoming. Fully functioning sewer and power systems were still a goal, and more street lights and paving had been delayed until 1954, something that Cecil and the other members of the Chamber of Commerce were said to be "highly disgusted" about.

Diane would also have been warned about the weather, which can change quickly and sometimes violently. Summer is an especially disorientating time in Fairbanks, because the sun barely sets for close to four months. This produces some amazingly large vegetables and flowers, and allows people to watch a midnight baseball game, but it's also when huge numbers of horror-movie size mosquitoes come out to bite.

Winter may be shorter, but it's still no picnic. More usually, darkness reigns for all but a few hours or so every day, and Fairbanks is also especially prone to ice fog, which occurs when the temperature is at least -40 degrees and the humidity close to 100%, and sees ice crystals freezing in mid-air. Advertisements for the Northward Building said that everyone living over the fourth floor would be above the level of the ice fog, so could always see the stars.

Winter can be notoriously brutal, but it was and is a major social season in Fairbanks. The Carnival of mushing, hockey, skating and skiing became a much-loved event after it was introduced in 1934, and in 1946 attendees could buy a raffle ticket for $1 and hope to win a brand new Cadillac, courtesy of Wells Alaska Motors of course.

Fun it may have been, but winter could also mean being indoors or snowed in for weeks or even months. A love for arts and crafts, books, puzzles and knitting would have been essential, and following in the footsteps of her artist mother, Diane took up ceramics lessons soon after arriving in town.

The unique weather conditions can have negative effects too, as periods of extended dark and light have been known to cause SAD (Seasonal Affective Disorder), a condition that can lead to depression.

That said, Fairbanks was one of the more vibrant cities in Alaska, and *Fighting for the Forty-Ninth Star* describes it as being a "small oasis of 1950s civilization." There was a radio station, two movie theaters, a bowling alley, scores of restaurants, bars, and even a drive-in liquor store — though television didn't arrive until 1955.

There was the *Fairbanks Daily News-Miner* too, but that was often barely a dozen pages long and always hungry for news, including about which notable locals were leaving town, who was receiving visitors, who was involved in family celebrations or events, or even if someone was feeling under the weather.

Events in America and the rest of the world were covered, but there was often a local story under the main headline. When Queen Elizabeth II was crowned in 1953 it was the headline of the day, but the sub-headline was a strong contrast, reading: "Fairbanks sizzles as Mercury Soars to 80s", while Edmund Hillary and Tensing Norgay's conquering of the 29,000-foot-high Mount Everest was one of the smaller stories underneath.

The city wasn't a shopper's paradise either, and with a train ride to Anchorage taking around 12 hours — and Juneau requiring a mammoth days-long bus, train and boat ride — it was common for people to fly down to Seattle, Portland, San Francisco or even Los Angeles to walk the aisles of luxury department stores, and enjoy the bright lights of a big city.

Air travel was often the best option. The Fairbanks International Airport opened in 1951, but many citizens, including Cecil, held pilot's licenses and had their own small planes — and still do. Children soon got used to flying, and in March 1951 the *FDNM* reported that Cecil and Diane's son Marquam, then just six-months old, had slept all the way home on a flight from Seattle, his escort being the owner of the Mecca Bar!

There were church, union and community clubs to join in Fairbanks, but as well as any segregation between black and white, they often delineated between the sexes. Many of them were men-only, or targeted at women (like the Homemaker Club or the Take Off Pounds Sensibly Club), so if you weren't a big joiner (or were the spouse of a notable local), they might have seemed more like a cheery obligation than chosen fun.

Making friends in a new city is always a challenge, and Judy Morris said that she found Diane to be "super nice," but also quiet. "She wasn't going out looking for many friends," she recalled, "because people were intimidated by her looks, and also her personality. She was plain old sophisticated."

As for other types of clubs, it would true to say that Fairbanks had a very flexible relationship with alcohol, too — at least unofficially. The Bone-Dry Law of 1918 came into force in the territory a couple of years before Prohibition, but it had little effect.

Back then 1st Avenue and 2nd Avenue (the latter of which was the first paved street in the city), were noted for being lined with drinking establishments. I visited the Mecca, which opened in 1945 and is the only remaining historical bar on 2nd Avenue, and also The Big International (known as The Big I), which is across the Chena River and opened in 1921, and began serving beer in 1933.

The *FDNM* was filled with advertisements for alcohol and the places you could get it too, and in 1953 the cocktail bars and nightclubs outnumbered the churches by four to one.

"At 5 o'clock in the morning you could probably go out there and get in trouble real easily," recalled Everett Hepp in the same 1982 interview, before adding "Not as well as I understand, over in Kodiak during the fishing season..."

In her memoir, Fairbanks native Sarah Crawford Isto writes that her high school principal had several convictions for DWI, and how functioning alcoholics were routinely tolerated, it being seen as a matter for the family. It took brawling in the street or passing out on the sidewalk to provoke any official action, or to join Alcoholics Anonymous. Fairbanks was a small town, and one day you might need that person's help.

While dancing girls and burlesque shows were often part of a night's entertainment during that era, a less welcome attraction for newly-arrived Diane was "The Line," a section of 4th Avenue where men could easily go for sex.

Since Gold Rush times it had been lined with formal and somewhat regulated brothels, and the women there worked without pimps, took regular blood tests, and were well dressed, wealthy, and often highly-respected (or at the very least tolerated), by police and the community. The military brass tried to keep it largely off-limits, especially since it also attracted illegal dice games and con men, but in a city so heavily-skewed towards men, it was seen as a necessary evil.

The Line was on its way out by the time she arrived, mainly due to civil nuisance lawsuits rather than local opposition, though a comment by local police that it was "closed, deserted and abandoned" in July 1953 was quickly rebuffed by a local councilor, who reported pay-offs to officers and said that the "sinister trade" was still happening. Jurists often refused to convict prostitutes anyway, for fear their female family members might be at risk from the many men in and around the city if it was to disappear.

I wondered what Diane thought about it, and how often it led to an uncomfortable — or even hostile — environment for her and other women in downtown Fairbanks.

Another interesting aspect of Alaska in the 1950s was its strong connection to Hawaii, though it wasn't the one I was told about when I popped into the Big International (Big I) pub in Fairbanks. Quite seriously, several different tourists over the years had told locals that they thought Alaska was an island. Why? Because, like Hawaii, it's always shown in a separate box on the TV weather reports.

Back in the 1950s both were pushing for statehood, and both were home to a large military presence. They were also been the only places within the continental US attacked by the Japanese in WWII. In the 1950s many Alaskans started to choose Hawaii for a vacation in part because it was close to the same flying time as, say, California. It was less geared towards mass tourism as well, and in January 1953, the *FDNM* gushed that Cecil and Diane had taken Marquam to Hawaii for six weeks to "soak up some of the silver moonlight and the gentle tropical breezes and the scene of a million flowers."

Flamboyant Hawaiian parties were often held in Fairbanks, too. I interviewed another grandchild of Cecil's, Cathi McMurrin, and she said that Cecil once flew the "princess or queen of Hawaii to Alaska," and a newspaper article dated July 1952 mentions the Wells held a luau (party) for 100 guests at their then-home on Illinois Street. Flowers, pineapples and coconuts were flown in from the islands, which was surely a huge expense, and guests were dressed in Aloha shirts and grass skirts.

"Striking blonde" Diane wore a green hula skirt over her bathing suit, as well as a carnation lei and orchids in her dyed hair, and there were hula dances and lessons, songs and music from Hawaiian servicemen stationed at local bases, and the rum and champagne flowed as guests ate roast suckling pig. In April 1953 the Lei Momi Hula Studio opened for students in the Northward

Building, and in July there was a Hawaiian luncheon held by the local Chamber of Commerce, when Diane and several other women danced for the crowd.

Both events were a big success, and while Cecil and Diane may have seemed like an unusual or unconventional match, hopes were high that wife number five might be his last one. However, Cathi McMurrin remembered that her mother said "a bunch of lava rock" had been sent to the luau to impress the guests, and it's actually considered very bad luck in Hawaiian culture to remove lava from the islands.

"And then Cecil was murdered," she said.

CHAPTER 3

"It's too late for Cecil"

Fairbanks, Alaska - Saturday October 17, 1953

Newspapers nicknamed her "the most beautiful woman in Alaska," but that day Diane Wells was called something very different: a victim.

It was soon after sunrise, around 7.15am, when a disorientated Diane crawled to apartment 812 and banged on the door of her neighbor at the Northward Building. Between tears, Diane told Alice Orahood a frightening story: in the small hours she had woken to find two men in the apartment she shared with Cecil and their three-year-old son Marquam — and then violence had come crashing into her life.

A bleary-eyed Orahood called Fairbanks Police, and led the sobbing Diane to a chair.

Officer Robert J. Templeton was dispatched into the very chilly morning, and on entering the darkened bedroom of the Wells' apartment 815 he noted that the curtains were open about a foot or so, and that "there was much blood on the pillow, and by my observation he (Cecil) had been beaten about the head with a heavy instrument." There was a distinctive injury above Cecil's right eye and, like Diane, his face was bloody.

Officer Templeton realized Cecil was dead, and took charge of what was now a crime scene. He ordered everyone present not to touch anything, though while the fireman used his handkerchief to turn on the bedroom light, the ambulance driver had already picked up Cecil's monogrammed black leather wallet in the corridor.

Mercifully, Marquam wasn't there, as he had been staying with his grandmother Frances in her apartment three floors below, so now Templeton called Dr. Donald McLean, the Wells' family doctor. He arrived at around 7.45am and made the first examination of 31-year-old Diane, who was "extremely distressed."

His report stated that both her lips had suffered severe tissue damage and swollen to twice their normal size. Her right eye was ballooning too (McLean noted a "severe contusion"), and her face and nose were bloody. He couldn't find any evidence that she had been unconscious, or for how long she might have been, though a severe blow could have caused it.

After the examination, the sobbing Diane insisted that her husband should go in the ambulance before her, even though McLean had already told her, as kindly as he could:

"It's too late for Cecil."

McLean officially declared Cecil dead, and again advised Diane that she should go to the hospital. She almost had to be manhandled onto a stretcher, and was eventually taken to St. Joseph's along with Sally Martin, a friend of hers who had just arrived.

At around 7.40am the city's outspoken Chief of Police E.V. Danforth and plainclothes Officer Stanley Zaverl arrived. Officer Templeton handed Danforth the wallet, which was empty save for a note about a house sale and Cecil's ID, and was sent back to the station to make out his report.

Clean-cut and rugged, the 39-year-old Danforth had barely been in the job five months, and he knew this was going to be an explosive case — but also a big opportunity. The pressure to bring Cecil's killer to account would be intense, because another high-profile crime, the murder of local businessman Tommy Wright back in January, seemed to have a similar modus operandi — and it was still unsolved.

ACTION IS NEEDED!

Wright's murder had increased the pressure on a high political level too. Alaska was trying to become the 49th US State, and law and order in

Fairbanks — and the territory as a whole — was a large obstacle they had to overcome.

In April, District Attorney Robert J. McNealy had described conditions at the Fairbanks city jail as a "filthy, foul, nightmare," proposed a raft of improvements, and used a shocking turn of phrase to describe Danforth's predecessor Ray Skelton as:

"An insane person, cutting throats with a butcher knife may be honest and sincere in a disillusioned way, but it's still fatal to the victims."

Skelton had resigned in disgrace after two men arrested for drunkenness had died in custody, one of them after Skelton had forced him, at the point of a tear-gas gun, to drink water, coffee, wine, and a sedative. Seven officers had quit or been fired by the unapologetic Skelton too, and insubordination and poor discipline was rampant.

In July, Alaska came under the control of the Bureau of Prisons, and the disgusted superintendent wrote in a report that Fairbanks staff were:

"Old, incompetent, untrustworthy and lazy jail guards whose loyalty to our new organization could not be depended on, and who showed very little interest in their work other than to draw their pay checks."

Danforth had a huge task ahead of him, but right now he took a breath and turned his attention to the dead man in the bedroom.

At St. Joseph's, nurses cleaned the blood away from Diane's mouth and nose, but her face was becoming even more swollen and discolored. Dr. McLean noted that "there was a remarkable change in her right eye. The swelling had increased by 50 percent and almost completely closed the palpebral slits, preventing easy examination of the eyeballs," and he concluded that this change meant that the original swelling had "not begun much over an hour and half" before his original exam.

At 8.15 Officer Charles Thrift arrived at the Wells' apartment and was ordered to photograph the crime scene and examine the apartment for fingerprints. The Fairbanks Police Department had no staff photographer, so a call was made to Fisher's Studio on Cushman Street, and when William Fisher entered the apartment, he immediately recognized a formal portrait of Diane and Marquam that he had taken.

Now he was there to capture another moment in that family's history, and walking into the bedroom he must have hesitated: it looked like Cecil was asleep, and that it would be easy to just wake him up.

This was echoed in Danforth's report of October 21, which said that Cecil was in the southwest bedroom, lying on his right side in apparent sleeping position. It also noted that there was no warmth to the body, and that he appeared to have been dead for some time. Blood had seeped out of his left ear, nose and mouth, and just above the right eye, and a great amount of blood had flowed to just below the waist, and coagulated up against the body.

The blood was only on the south side of the bed, with "numerous, small blood spots on the head of bed, and extending upwards to a height of approx. 6 feet." Danforth also speculated that Cecil had been struck over the right eye, but the large amount of bleeding meant he would have to wait for the autopsy. For now, Zaverl and he continued to search the Wells' apartment for anything that might indicate a robbery, which was the apparent motive.

Elsewhere, a six-foot tall man was driving south in his 1949 Pontiac.

Johnny Warren was a 33-year-old African-American singer and musician who played drums, bass, piano and guitar in many of the local clubs, and also worked at the Piggly Wiggly grocery store on 2nd Avenue. He was heading to Oakland, California, a journey of some 3,000 miles, and was said to be in the company of two other people, though not his pregnant wife Clara, who was reportedly ill and unable to make the trip.

They had already passed through Canadian customs at Tok Junction, some 200 miles from Fairbanks, and were on the famous Alaska Highway.

A superhuman engineering effort of 11,000 servicemen (including around 4,000 badly-treated African-American soldiers), and then later 6,000 civilian workers, the road was created as part of the war effort. It was completed in eight months instead of the planned two years, and runs from Dawson Creek in British Columbia, Canada, to Delta Junction in Alaska.

Fairbanks is 96 miles from Delta Junction, but nevertheless many consider it the last stop. I examined Milepost 1523, a marker for that "unofficial end of the Alaska Highway", and wondered what Johnny had been thinking as he started the long journey down to Oakland.

Today, a trip along the 1,400 or so miles of the Highway is recommended by glossy travel magazines — perhaps with a group of friends in a high-end RV — but back then it was a serious dusty and/or muddy undertaking. One of the first things I learned on arriving in Fairbanks was that every vehicle, including rental cars, has cracks and chips in the windshield. They happen so often while driving here that it's not worth replacing or repairing them until things get really bad.

Earlier that cloudy morning, several people had seen Johnny at the Northward, and he and his passengers had left town soon after. That might have seemed suspicious to some, but then Deputy U.S. Marshal Frank Wirth received a tip from Tommy Wright's son that Diane had been "fond" of Johnny.

Wright's son would want have wanted Cecil's killers caught, as they could have been the men who killed his father earlier in the year, and so locating Johnny became a priority.

His name and license plate #36143 went out on the wires.

CHAPTER 4

Witness Statements

The District Attorney's office was in the Northward Building (and still is), but it was locked and dark as police officers began their door-to-door interviews of the residents and staff, and tried to locate anyone who had been there the night of the murder.

The Northward Building cost $2,500,000 to build (around $24m today), and the grand opening of the memorable "ultra-modern", steel-framed, aluminum-sheathed building took up several pages of the local paper in February 1952. At a rent of $135 per month it was attractive to potential residents of a certain type, and it was no coincidence that Wells Alaska Motors welcomed it with an advertisement in that same paper.

Cecil, Diane and young Marquam moved in a few months later, and took two apartments, 814 and 815, which were converted so there were two bedrooms and bathrooms with an adjoining door. They had been living on Illinois Street in an area that's still known as Garden Island, and their three bedroom, two bath home had quickly found a buyer.

Leaving this larger, detached house meant losing a garden, but moving across the Chena River to the glittering "skyscraper" seemed like an obvious choice. Not only was Cecil's dealership on that side of the river, but so were many of his political and civil concerns. When he became president of the local Chamber he predicted that "Nothing can stop Fairbanks until it takes its place as Alaska's number one city," and with statehood always on the horizon, it seemed obvious that the Wells family should be at the new symbolic center of the busy downtown.

The 210 units were equivalent to a big city hotel, or what we'd know today as a serviced facility, and it had a "pretty, blonde" elevator operator, maid service, laundry, seamstress, stenographer and even an in-house detective who watched over the businesses on street level.

These included a cocktail lounge, coffee shop, barber shop, a drug store, liquor store, the Bank of Fairbanks (of which Cecil was a director), and more, which meant you didn't ever have go out in the cold or snow to run your daily life. Even the basement parking was heated, and then as now, access to the apartments was for residents only.

With Cecil's mother living in the Northward too, the Wellses would have a babysitter on hand so they could enjoy the nightlife close by, and Diane was now closer to the stores and restaurants.

Also, the apartment was relatively small, so she might have an excuse not to host ladies' "socials" or afternoon teas, which were a big part of life for the women in town, whether you liked them or not.

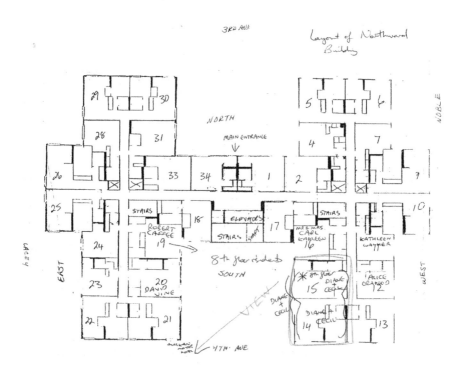

As law enforcement spread out around the Northward, the first person to be interviewed was Alice Orahood. Despite living opposite the Wells, the police report noted she was "not a personal friend," and she said she heard nothing unusual before Diane woke her. Several other residents, including Cecil's mother, said they were undisturbed too.

Apart from Diane, the last confirmed person to see Cecil alive was airline executive Herb Mensing, who had come for dinner before Cecil and Diane went to see the Robert Stack movie *War Paint* at The Empress. He had already flown back to Anchorage though, and was never extensively interviewed. It seems police didn't consider him to be involved in any way.

One resident, Fred Stevens, asked to see Danforth outside of the Northward, where he told him that just after midnight on the 17th he heard a voice that sounded like a child crying "Don't hit me daddy, don't hit me daddy." The cries apparently went on for 10 minutes, and Stevens was so alarmed that he even "hollered into the ventilator to leave the kid alone," after which the noise stopped. Was this Marquam crying, or another child somewhere in the building?

There were similar reports from other residents. The Hollebecks in apartment 715, directly below the Wells, said they were woken around 7am "by the sound of something hitting the floor," and that "I thought it was the little boy jumping around. I listened at the vent in the kitchen and heard a voice say, 'it hurts, or it's hurt'." Carl Kahleen lived in 816, next door to the Wells, and his statement was brief but potentially damning:

"My wife knows a lot about the squabbles the Wells had from hearing them through the vent."

The Fleiders in 714, also directly below the Wells, said that one evening a couple of weeks earlier they heard "loud screaming, and a man berating a woman for about 15 minutes. Then we heard sobbing." Their guests that night, also residents of the Northward, heard it too.

In the 1950s, the idea of domestic abuse was almost alien. Police rarely intervened in such matters, and even today it is still excused, ignored and even tolerated by its desperate victims, and law enforcement, with the term "Domestic Violence" not even used in modern context until 1973. Many years later, Judy Morris recalled that she had once seen a bruise on Diane's face, but when she asked about it, Diane replied: "Oh, that's just Cecil."

As for punishing children, the odd smack (or worse) to a disobedient child was accepted in those times; it was even considered good parenting.

Social roles were very defined at the time, with men almost exclusively the breadwinners, and women the homemakers who provided the care and comfort. That wasn't true in every case, but discussions with members of the Wells family did seem to indicate that Cecil's fathering skills weren't his strongest asset.

Judy also remembered that Cecil's incentive for her to help him domestically was a brand new vacuum cleaner, a luxurious appliance not common to many homes at the time:

"He handed it to me and said: 'Here's the vacuum cleaner, so now you have to live up to your end.'"

More seriously, on the occasion when she saved her half-sister Ethel from a beating by Cecil, she recalled that he said:

"Well, I'm just going to go kill myself then, you ladies can support yourselves."

Though it represented 1960 onward, the relationships and social attitudes portrayed on HBO's long-running series "Mad Men" were very similar to the 1950s. This was a time when many men expected to come home from the office to find domestic bliss: dinner, a cocktail, a freshly-scrubbed home, a perfectly made-up wife, and perfectly-behaved children waiting sleepily for a kiss goodnight.

However, it's important to note that the witness interviews were conducted with many other people, several of whom were in close proximity to the Wells' apartment, and they all heard nothing that night. Not a shout, not a cry, not a sudden noise, not even a gunshot. When Diane was later told how Cecil had died, she also said: "I didn't hear a shot."

No one in the apartments on the opposite side of the building to 815 happened to be at their window at the right time to see anything either, though it was later revealed there was an evening when several people were deliberately peeping into the Wells apartment.

It's also possible that it wasn't Cecil, Diane or Marquam that people had heard arguing or crying. Neighborly spats, a desire to tell the authorities what they think they want to hear, a sense of guilt that they should have been more observant, or simply a desire to be involved in the drama: all of these can affect what witnesses tell police.

As for outside the Northward, foot traffic on the streets was probably non-existent in the pre-dawn light. Apartment 815 was angled on one of the inner sides of the "H" shape, and when I managed to briefly get into 815 and look out of the window, and then look back up from the street, it was clear anyone could have missed a momentary muzzle flash, even if there had been one.

I was surprised to see that no one from apartment 813 had been interviewed, though chances are they had little or nothing to add when they were spoken to at a later stage. Nor did the building's two janitors, who had been at the work around 6-7am, though a new employee at the Northward Bar said that a little after closing time, perhaps around 2 or 3am, he saw a man sitting in the lobby who was "waiting for a friend to change dimes." What that means isn't clear, and after this statement it read on the report "(Not checked)".

This part of downtown was very much a place for night birds and partyers, and Jouida Gail and Virginia Rowe who lived in 434 had been out for the evening with two male friends, who left at 5am after what was a very late midnight snack. The two women added that William Colombany, a ballroom dancing teacher, called them at 4am, but perhaps because they had company, he didn't join them. They imagined Colombany had been in his apartment/studio, 231, as such late-night calls from him were apparently common.

Colombany stated that he had been with Cecil and Grace Hoitt in the Northward Bar earlier that evening around 6pm, then took Grace and a female friend home before driving back. He was then "in and out" of the building until 9pm, when he went to apartment 726 (occupant not mentioned), then to the Talk of the Town club, where he stayed until 4am before getting a ride home with his friend Louis Krize.

"I know the Wells very well," Colombany told the investigating officer, and it was true that he and his employee Jouida Gail were good friends, especially with Diane. In fact, his relationship with Diane came under increasing scrutiny in the following months.

In the 1950s ballroom dancing was a popular hobby, and after reading an advertisement about the many benefits it apparently offered, Cecil and Diane signed up for weekly lessons. The teacher was Colombany, a man of medium height and wavy, black hair, and the trio quickly found they had a lot in common.

"Bill" was new in town from Anchorage, and when they learned he was from Guatemala, Cecil and Diane undoubtedly talked to him about their trip there in 1952. Colombany subsequently joined Cecil in the Chamber of Commerce, and also supported the Community Hotel.

Colombany said that he didn't hear about the murder until Jouida called him around 8-8.30am, but later police would look again at his recall of that morning's events, and he would be questioned about it in court.

Another prominent local couple were interviewed. Construction company owner Lloyd Martin was a business partner of Cecil's, and had known him for close to a decade. They didn't live in the Northward, but Lloyd owned it. He however had little to offer about the morning of the murder, as he had arrived in town on a Pan-Am flight just before 6am, when his wife Sally had picked him up at the airport.

Sally then got two calls from a "hysterical" Diane around 7.30am, the second saying that Cecil had been "hurt," and after dressing she went over to see what had happened. She arrived just as Diane was leaving for the hospital, and heard her tell police that the front door was locked during the night.

It would be natural to assume that Sally joined Diane in the ambulance, but instead she braved the low 20 degrees temperature and walked the few blocks to St. Joseph's Hospital, crossing Cushman Street Bridge en route. Much later, an unpublished memoir would wonder why she did that. Perhaps there was simply no space in the vehicle — or maybe there was another reason.

CHAPTER 5

"Shut up, or I will kill you"

A few minutes after 11am, detective Zaverl interviewed Diane while she lay in her hospital bed. Another officer stood guard outside the door as Grace Hoitt, who had come to sit with Diane after Sally Martin left, excused herself.

Diane explained that the night before around 7pm, Cecil had called up from the Northward Bar to say that he was bringing Herb Mensing up for dinner. Diane was irritated by this last-minute decision as it meant she had to go out to buy some more hamburger, plus she and Cecil had originally planned to go out to see a movie. Cecil had brought a couple unexpectedly to dinner the previous night, too.

After arriving at the apartment Cecil asked for a drink of bourbon, and Mensing said that Cecil had already had four Old Fashioned cocktails (though the bar waiter "Trigger" confirmed it was actually three).

After dinner at around 8.55pm, Diane put on her coat to give Herb the hint it was time to leave, and she and Cecil walked with him to the Nordale Hotel, where they parted ways. After they had seen *War Paint* Cecil and Diane walked home, had a drink, then Cecil went to bed. Diane read the newspaper for a while before joining him, and then was "dreaming."

Her statement follows verbatim from the report:

"I woke up and saw a silhouette of a man standing at the foot of the bed on Cecil's side. I nudged Cecil and then I pinched him and he said what's the matter — or — what do you want. Then the man moved towards Cecil and I rushed out of bed into the living room. I bumped into another man, and I was so surprised and terrified that I didn't say anything. He grabbed me by the arm and put his hand over my mouth. He had gloves on, because I

25

remember I tried to bite his hand. He said "shut up or I will kill you." He reached for a flowerpot and hit me with it. He reached for another flowerpot but I passed out before it hit me. I think the bathroom light was on. It seemed that I was out only a little while. It was lighter when I woke up on my hands and knees. I went across the hall and banged on the door for help."

She described a "feeling of fear," and certainly paid the price for fighting back, saying that she "saw stars" after she was hit in the head.

Understandably, the *FDNM* lavished excited coverage on what was a huge story.

CECIL WELLS MURDERED IN BEDROOM; WIFE, DIANA, FOUND BADLY BEATEN

Underneath the headline was a formal portrait of Cecil, and under that the Fisher Studio photograph of Diane and Marquam, the same one that was in the apartment. It was puzzling that she was called "Diana" rather than Diane, though research revealed that she had been known by several different names throughout her life.

The newspaper report contained a couple of errors. Firstly, it said that Cecil was 51 years old, when he was in fact less than two weeks shy of that birthday. More seriously, it noted that Cecil's skull had been crushed "by some sort of an instrument" and "there was no evidence that he had been shot." Danforth was quoted too. He dismissed the empty wallet found in the corridor because Cecil never usually carried cash, and said that robbery was apparently not the motive for the crime.

He further noted that a number of valuable items had not been touched, and that he had certain "clues" he could not make public at this time. He added that Diane's statements about the night of the murder had been of little use.

A few days later on October 20, the *FDNM* ran a photograph of the injured Diane "Three days after the terror of her sudden attack," and it started by listing her current condition:

"Her eyes are shiny black, her jaw is puffed, her nose is lumped out of shape, her lips are swollen and thick, and there are lacerations scattered on her face and scalp."

Lying on the sofa in their Northward apartment, she had spoken to *FDNM* editor Jack Ryan about what happened, and added several more details.

She said that the man who killed Cecil was tall and slender, and when she woke up he was bending over Cecil's clothes on a chair, maybe looking for his wallet. As soon as Cecil replied to her urgings to wake up, this man then "made for him." Diane had run from the room by then, and she said the man she ran into in the hallway was also tall and fairly heavy.

After she was grabbed and hit with the flowerpot, she said that it seemed "lighter somehow," and after regaining consciousness she didn't call the police, but went to get help from the neighbors. She returned to the bedroom to check on Cecil, and then tried to call Dr. Paul Haggland, who wasn't home, so she tried calling some friends:

"I wanted someone to come and help me, and then they took me to hospital."

Diane was sure both intruders wore quilted or padded jackets, and admitted that "she doesn't know why, but she has a definite impression that the man who grabbed her was white." How she knew this wasn't clear, as she didn't see any faces, not even an inadvertent glimpse of skin on the arm that was around her neck, but either way, the question of race had now entered the story.

She also had a theory that the prowlers had been in the apartment before (a man she found "adjusting the radiator"), and targeted Cecil because they thought he carried a lot of money. She also hinted that the thieves might have gained access via 814, perhaps with a spare key, though police had already said they doubted there was a key that opened all the apartment doors.

She also mentioned that 815's front door special Schlage multi-lock wasn't "pick proof." She had once locked herself out and a locksmith had opened it in a second she said, though at this time all five keys to the Schlage were accounted for. Also, it wasn't clear if their door had a safety chain, or whether it had been forced to get inside.

Diane then "carefully" described her last few hours with Cecil.

Arriving back at the Northward they met neighbor Kathleen Walker in the elevator, and joked about being thirsty; *War Paint* was a Western with a plot point about running out of water.

They arrived back at the apartment at 11.20pm and Cecil joked: "speaking of being thirsty," and went to the kitchen. She didn't see what he did before he went to bed, but she made herself a drink. She then took a "pill which I am supposed to take before going to bed," and stayed up to read the newspaper. Cecil shouted to ask her when she was coming to bed, and she didn't know what time she actually retired for the night.

The pill she mentioned was for a stomach disorder, which Diane said she had been suffering for weeks. She had been placed on a special diet too, but she broke it when Herb came for dinner, something that apparently gave her vomiting spells, and she later rushed to the bathroom. Cecil joined her and asked "What's the matter honey? That'll teach you to eat fried meat for dinner."

He gave her a pair of his pajamas to wear instead of her now-soiled night clothes, though she said she had no idea when this occurred, and didn't wake up again until she saw someone at the end of their bed. Cecil probably didn't respond to her panicked nudges and urgings because he slept heavily and snored, especially when he lay on his back, and Diane "would always nudge him to roll over."

Also, despite what Danforth had said, Diane was positive that some "valuable items" were missing. She and Cecil were due to go to Anchorage the next day for an airport dedication, and she had been planning to take an amethyst necklace, ring and bracelet set, valued together at $625 (around $5,500 today). They had now vanished.

Diane also told Ryan that she was not satisfied with the police investigation, and that Chief Danforth had ignored her requests to bring in the FBI, who were based in Anchorage but nominally had a satellite office in Fairbanks, allegedly replying that it was out of their jurisdiction.

There already seemed to be a question over what had happened, or at least what Diane had said happened, but for now the death of one of Fairbanks' pioneers was just starting to send shock waves throughout the territory. It even knocked the opening of Anchorage's new $11m airport, which was also marking the 50th anniversary of the Wright Brothers first powered flight, off the front page of the *Anchorage Daily News*.

As the story began to be picked up by newspapers across the States, Theodore "Ted" Stevens, the newly-appointed U.S. District Attorney in Fairbanks, complained that Danforth was keeping the DA, the US Marshals and the Territorial Police out of the loop and "going it alone."

Born in Indianapolis and only 29 years old, the bespectacled and formal-looking Stevens was a graduate of UCLA and Harvard. He had only been with the local Collins & Clasby law firm less than six months, and there were worries about his trial skills and his experience. He was also new in town, which was always a challenge, but Stevens was clearly ambitious.

Starting work on September 1, he was the youngest DA in Fairbanks history and inherited a backlog of 100 cases — but he came out guns blazing. From the outset he worked long hours, actively chased down violations of liquor, drugs and prostitution, and was said to pack a pistol when he accompanied the US Marshals. It was a claim he later said was exaggerated, though it didn't hurt his image.

His early support for the defunct Crime Squad (or "T-Squad") caused a stir too. Staffed by members from the city police, territorial police and marshals' office, they dealt with felonies and had a clear mission to keep any residents from being "robbed, slugged or shot." Stevens was quoted as saying that the Crime Squad was "the tool to dig out vice by the roots."

It had foundered after a few months though, largely because of resistance from Danforth. The small and overburdened Territorial Police had soon dropped out too, and a rare veto by Fairbanks' Mayor over a proposed gambling tax that would have helped fund them was a killer blow. Despite the Squad's success they were never popular with the locals either, who often turned a blind eye to illegal activities, especially gambling.

The ferocious beginning to his tenure put noses out of joint, but Stevens had found an ally in the pro-statehood *Fairbanks Daily News-Miner*, who urged harmony and said that Danforth's "uncooperative attitude isn't strengthening the hand of law and order in this area," and that "no individual was above the welfare of the public."

Stevens knew that solving the murder of Cecil Wells could define his career — or end it before it had begun — but at the moment Danforth was keeping him at arm's length. Danforth had allies too, including Reuben Tarte, Cecil's close friend and business partner, who had flown in from Seattle to make the funeral arrangements.

The City Manager pleaded that everyone should "quit worrying about who's on top," and how Fairbanks "had officers all over the place... and (that) there was much repetition and confusion" during the previous investigation of Tommy Wright's murder in January 1953.

Bar owner Wright had also been murdered in his home, and his wife Eleanor told the inquest that they had found two masked men waiting for them. The thieves had used a glass cutter to gain access to the house, then helped themselves to champagne and whisky while they lay in wait. When the Wrights returned there was a struggle, and one of the men, who was wearing a red Halloween mask, opened fire at point-blank range with a .38.

Wright had been armed, as the *FDNM* reported that he had an "inkling" he was in danger of being robbed and had actually asked for a police escort, but that night had decided a ride home with an employee would be sufficient. This proved to be a deadly mistake, and it seemed he was shot before he could draw his weapon.

The Wright's house had been thoroughly ransacked, and the liquor bottles were taken to be examined for fingerprints, though they were no help in the investigation. Wright wasn't carrying the takings from his three bars, and the thieves only got away with the $20 Eleanor had in her purse.

The Wright and Wells crime were very similar, and they reminded some people of another early-morning home invasion that took place in December 1951, when Piggly Wiggly store owner and acting mayor Earl Hausmann and his wife were attacked at home by two "bandits" with a machine gun and a pistol.

They took $200 from Hausmann's wallet and forced him and his wife to drive back to the store and open the office safe, from which they took over

$2,000. No one was injured, but as in the Wright case, no arrests were made.

The witness descriptions from the Hausmanns, Eleanor Wright and now Diane Wells were all rather vague, though there was agreement that the men were 5ft 8 and 5ft 11, and, though their faces were covered by woolen hats, turned-up collars, masks or mufflers, that they were definitely white. At the time of the Wright murder, the *FDNM* even speculated:

"Could it be that they are the same bandits in all cases, and they are well-known people in this city, and would be identified immediately if seen by their victims?"

The duo had a taste for liquor, never left behind any fingerprints, and were certainly organized even if they didn't score big money, so this panic-inducing statement probably made everyone suspicious of their neighbors, let alone strangers, and the editorial added that several men who felt they might be targets were considering moving elsewhere.

Despite a reward of close to $3,000 (over $29,000 today) put up by local businessman and the efforts of several branches of law enforcement, no one had been arrested for the Wright murder.

"I don't want that to happen this time," stated the City Manager.

The pressure was piling onto Danforth now. After all, rich businessmen like Tommy Wright and Cecil Wells weren't killed in their homes in a place that was good enough to join the 48 states of America.

CHAPTER 6

The Autopsy

On the afternoon of October 17, Coroner Dr. Paul Haggland was summoned to the Memorial Chapel funeral home to examine Cecil's corpse. He began the autopsy on the stiffened, blood-encrusted body at 2.40pm, and almost immediately discovered a bullet hole:

"On the left side of the skull, 1/4 inch in diameter, 3/4 of an inch behind the ear and an inch above, there is a smooth round hole with a burn margin.... A probe was passed thru the hole on the left side of the skull in the parietal region thru the brain cavity and then out thru the right supraorbital region.... The brain was removed in toto and it was found that the bullet has traversed the brain and disrupted the brain tissue of the floor of the fourth ventricle and lateral ventricles, passed out through the right frontal lobe and in its course disrupted the blood vessels at the base of the brain."

Haggland then opened the abdomen and found little unusual. The kidneys were normal, but the liver showed some changes which "go with modern living," and there was some incompletely digested food in the stomach, a specimen of which was kept to help determine the time of death.

A ring was removed from Cecil's fourth digit — perhaps his wedding ring — and because it had blood on it, it was carefully put into an envelope. It then seemed to disappear, as I didn't find any mention of it in the police or FBI files.

When the bedclothes were removed and shaken, a cartridge case was found. It too was put into an envelope by the gloved Haggland, and a call was immediately made to Danforth to begin a search for the bullet at the crime scene. It was found embedded in Cecil's pillow and was identified as a .380, which meant that the weapon was a semi-automatic pistol, where bullets are fired from a clip, rather than the circular chamber of a revolver. I wondered too if the pillow had muffled the sound of the shot.

In simple terms, the entry wound had been just above Cecil's left ear, and the bullet came out the right side of his skull at the supraorbital ridge (the eyebrow ridge). But then how close was the killer when he — or she — opened fire? The term "burn margin" definitely suggests that the gun was close enough for the discharge flame to mark Cecil's skin, but the specific murder weapon wasn't known at the time, and it's one of a number of factors that could affect the accuracy of such an estimate.

An entry wound surrounded by dotted particles of discharged gunpowder, an effect known as tattooing or stippling, could mean the muzzle was as close as six inches, but Haggland doesn't use those exact terms. Alternatively, a small hole with a black/blue mark around can indicate the gun was fired two feet or more from the victim, and it's likely Haggland felt the distance should be left officially undetermined. Those who could read between the lines would probably make their own conclusions.

Either way, the gun certainly wasn't placed against Cecil's head and fired. Pressure changes when the barrel of a semi-automatic is pressed against a surface can prevent firing, and anyway, that kind of entry wound is shaped like a jagged star. It made no difference anyway, as Cecil probably didn't even wake up before he was killed.

Haggland finished the autopsy in less than an hour, and he then wrote to a Seattle pathologist about the contents of Cecil's stomach, and how much use it could be in medico-legal terms. The pathologist referred him to the book *Homicide Investigation*, which noted the "great importance" of examination of the stomach contents in fixing the time of death.

If stomach contents are present a pathologist may well be able to tell "with reasonable accuracy of what the last meal consisted," it says, explaining further that it's usually emptied of food between four to six hours after a meal has been eaten. If a stomach is found to be well filled with food, then death happened shortly after a meal, and if entirely empty, it happened "at least four to six hours" earlier.

Another book, *Physiological Basis of Medical Practice*, notes some interesting facts about human digestion including that a meal largely consisting of fats leaves the body quickest, followed by one of carbohydrates, with a meat-based meal taking the longest.

They note that an "ordinary mixed meal" usually leaves the human stomach in three to four-and-a-half hours, and that a "test meal" is usually evacuated in around two hours, with fluids and semi-fluids starting to leave the stomach almost immediately. The study listed how long bread and lean meat took, with olive oil taking the longest time; after over four hours, only 60% of it was removed.

As for his own experience of autopsies after sudden death, the pathologist believed that "only very small quantities of gruel-like material in which no specific food particles can be identified is found in the stomach after 4 hours."

Cecil and Diane did have dinner the night before he was killed, and Diane also said that they'd had a late meal of chicken from their icebox after arriving home around 11.20pm. Unless it was an especially fatty cut of meat, it should have been out of Cecil's stomach in around four hours, making the time of death 3am at the earliest. Dr. McLean's preliminary report to Danforth said it was later, between 5.30 and 6.30am, and this matched his assessment that the swelling on Diane's face began 90-120 minutes before his original examination of her.

However, Haggland's autopsy was frustratingly vague about the incompletely digested food he had taken a specimen of, both in terms of how large that food was and how large a specimen he took, let alone any sense of what it might have been. It seems sensible then to assume that the specimen was of a "gruel-like" substance, though that didn't stop it being raised in court during the inquest on Cecil's death.

At this stage in the investigation Danforth would have been happy, even if he had been over-confident in stating publicly that Cecil had been shot; he wouldn't have been able to see the exit wound, and Cecil's head injuries and the internal bleeding that made the skin on his head look black and blue could have fooled anyone.

Now he and his officers had fingerprints, bloodstains, the fatal bullet and its cartridge, and even a potential suspect, Johnny Warren, on the run. It wasn't until a week later that many people first heard about that suspect, when the *FDNM* coyly reported that he was a "local entertainer who was friendly with the principals in this case. The man, who is colored, left town the morning after the crime traveling down the Alaska highway by car."

Most locals could easily guess who that was, though confusingly, the report continued to say that the police "didn't consider him to be a very likely suspect, however." Suspect or not, Johnny Warren was still on the road, his exact location unknown.

Diane stayed overnight in the hospital, and now she needed clothes and personal possessions for herself and Marquam, even if returning to apartment 815 was undoubtedly going to be traumatic. Danforth didn't make it any easier, dramatically handing the keys to her while he stood like a sentinel outside the front door.

In many ways the apartment was still like she had always known it, though some items would have been removed for evidence, and it's doubtful there would have been any cleaning or tidying of what was now a crime scene. The blood-stained mattress in their marital bedroom was still there, though she didn't go in: she only visited Marquam's bedroom to get some clothes and toys for him.

Also, there were her soiled night clothes, which raised the question of possible GSR (gunshot residue). Danforth told the coroner's inquest they "were lying near the door of the Wells' bathroom, but that he had not seen them himself, and they had not been recovered."

Perhaps no one thought they were important, or just didn't want to touch the sticky, smelly pile, but now there were questions about Diane's story. Surely they should have been collected and tested along with the replacement pajamas she had worn? It seems that the night clothes were never retrieved, and it's likely they were washed, which meant that any evidence on them went down into the drains of Fairbanks, or they were simply thrown in the trash.

As Diane stepped gingerly around the stain on the living room carpet, she must have felt she was under a microscope.

Danforth had been openly dismissive of her account of the night of Cecil's murder, and watched while she took a quick inventory. He later told reporters that she was "badly broken up" and nervous about returning to the apartment, which might account for her saying that some other costume jewelry pieces were missing, but were found soon after.

Now she said that just one item was unaccounted for, a red precious stone in a heart shape, but then she looked into a secret compartment in a nest of tables.

After pulling out a checkbook she said "Oh, it's gone," and explained that there had been $1,000 cash tucked in it. It was money Cecil regularly left for Diane and Marquam when he "flew his plane or made a trip," and she had put it there herself — though how the thieves would have known about this secret compartment wasn't clear.

After leaving the apartment, Diane and Marquam began a temporary, couch-surfing lifestyle. Cecil had surely looked after the family's accounts, and since there were no ATMs and even the recently-introduced Diners' Club card was only valid at certain establishments, she was suddenly in need of money for everything from food to legal fees.

She did not have her own income and may not have been a co-signer on the Wells bank account either, so now she was relying on others. Neighbors and friends like Thelma Walker helped out or bought some of Diane's furniture, which seemed to indicate that the $1,000 taken from the secret compartment wasn't found after all, or didn't last very long. Walker added that Diane was depressed at the time, and had tried to jump out the window.

Diane gave a key for the apartment to her friend Bill Colombany, who helped with the furniture sale and later collected more clothes for Marquam, but this was the last time she ever went into her family home.

CHAPTER 7

The Forensics

In June 2018, almost a year after I had requested it, the FBI file on Cecil Wells' murder arrived at my Los Angeles apartment. It was 133 pages in length, and included handwritten notes, draft letters and lab work sheets. It was interesting to see what J. Edgar Hoover and his men had decided to invest time and resources on back in 1953/1954, and how the investigation went on for so many years.

A number of items from the crime scene at the Northward Building had been taken to the Fairbanks police station in City Hall, a squat, two storey, concrete art deco building, where they were labeled Q1, Q2 etc. before being shipped 4,000 miles to the FBI for analysis.

.380 caliber slug (or bullet) taken from rubber pillow (Q1)

.380 caliber shell case (or cartridge) found in bedding (Q2)

A water glass found in the kitchen sink about one fourth full of whisky & water

4/5 of a qt. Bottle of Johnny (sic) Walker Scotch Whisky one fourth full

4/5 empty quart bottle - Smirnoff Vodka

Pressure cooker button cont. small amount of blood on it

1 or 2 clay flowerpots in pieces along with a quantity of the earth, roots of plant

1 pr. black high heeled dress shoes (woman)

Navy type blue knitted wool stocking cap found at cab parking area on First Ave. 7.55am October by officer Templeton

Foam rubber pillow and two inner and one outer pillow cases

Sample of blood taken from the mattress which was under victim

Sample of blood taken from living room carpet

Sample (minute quantity) scraped from bedroom wall East side

Before they were shipped, Danforth ordered the pressure cooker button and shoes (both of which seemed to have blood on them) sent to the local Fairbanks Medical and Surgical Clinic for testing, but a negative result made this decision a mistake that cost time and money. As for the stocking cap, Diane had said that one of the men that attacked her wore one, so Danforth asked the owner of a cab company that worked out of the Northward to send him a list of the employees that were working that night: presumably they all checked out.

The report that Danforth wrote on October 23 was perhaps the first time he had communicated with FBI Director Hoover, and he briefly explained the details of case number 95-51424-1, writing that Cecil had died between 12.30 and 7am, a wider time span than the scientific evidence had suggested, and that a .380 caliber bullet was used.

He described Diane's injuries as not serious, and wanted to know what blood types they had found, what make of gun fired the .380 slug, and whether there were any fingerprints on the bottles, water glass, pillow case and pressure cooker. He also asked for information about any hair in the wool cap, though whether that meant there was some present wasn't clear.

Q1 and Q2 were the most important items on that evidence list, and that .380 caliber bullet and cartridge case made the journey to and from Washington, D.C., several times over the next few years.

Also taken as evidence from the scene was the book *The Prophet* by Kahlil Gibran. It was found on a table near the kitchen, and page 46 had the bottom turned up as an impromptu marker; there were small smears of nail polish on that page too. Diane had said she read the paper before she went to bed, but this was probably a book she was reading at the time too, as it certainly didn't seem Cecil's style.

A few weeks later Danforth would describe this book as the final "gap" in the investigation, and said that Diane had asked for it to be retrieved from the apartment before she went to hospital on the morning of the murder.

A collection of prose poetry fables about a prophet, Almustafa, who is about to take a ship home after spending a dozen years living in Orphalese, it was first published in 1923 and in the 1950s, 1960s and even 1970s it was extraordinarily popular, and still is today. It has sold millions of copies, and was even brought to life as an animated movie in 2014 thanks to the efforts of actress/producer Salma Hayek.

I ordered a copy, and saw that chapters were titled Love, Marriage, Joy and Sorrow, Pain and Self-Knowledge, Houses, Work and more. I quickly turned to page 46 and found that it was between the chapters on Crime and Punishment and Freedom.

Diane might have read the words "What laws shall you fear if you dance but stumble against no man's iron chains?" before she went to bed, but going back a couple of pages into the Crime and Punishment chapter was this quote:

"If any of you would bring to judgment the unfaithful wife, let him also weigh the heart of her husband in scales, and measure his soul with measurements."

A few paragraphs later was the quote that Danforth noted had been marked:

"What penalty lay you upon him who slays in the flesh yet is himself slain in the spirit?"

As Danforth's six-page report came to an end, he noted a few more things including: "Rumors, information and some evidence link several well-known and prominent Fairbanks residents with Wells's wife in some way or other."

It was only a sentence, but the subtext was very clear, and it indicated Danforth's thinking about what may have been a factor in the murder.

He also listed the Fairbanks officers who had worked the case "before the Marshals Office and Territorial Police were requested to aid," a few words that hid a lot of anger and resentment, as Danforth was furious that the investigation was being given to the US Marshals. It was just the beginning of a bruising battle between various personalities and agencies, though hopes were high that with so many people on the case, this could be looked back upon as the ideal example of inter-agency cooperation that saw the murderer or murderers brought swiftly to justice.

A joint statement from these agencies warned about "false rumors implicating innocent people," though others were already impatient for results. A group of local businessmen suggested that $10,000 could be raised to fund a private investigation, but the *FDNM* reported that local law enforcement thought a criminologist might not want to "risk his reputation" by trying to solve a crime where the leads have grown cold - and this was barely a week after the murder.

"Without attempting to suggest any particular person as being the person who killed Cecil Wells," Danforth then wrote his conclusions. He mentioned the open curtains in the bedroom, and that Alice Orahood saw the Wells' living room light was on. He also mentioned that "No dirt or other foreign matter" was found on Diane, and the "thump of some thing hitting the floor" heard at around 7am. He also noted that the pathological tests were forthcoming on the contents of Cecil's stomach.

A couple of days later, two more items were added to the boxes to be sent to the FBI. The first was a cellophane envelope containing two small pieces of fur or wool threads that, Danforth wrote, "We have not been able to figure. A larger quantity was found on victims' pillow in front of his face. Victim was shot thru back of head." The second envelope contained pieces of the flowerpot or pots, which seemed to have a spot of blood on them, and he asked the FBI to identify the blood type:

"We are trying to establish who beat Dianne (sic) Wells, if victim was injured in any way other than being shot, and if she was hit with her shoes, flowerpots & pressure cooker."

Even in a struggle it was odd to imagine Diane being attacked with shoes, flowerpots and part of a pressure cooker, but Danforth was already suspicious about her, and seemed to be looking for some physical evidence to back him up.

As for the murder weapon, the police had thoroughly searched apartment 815, looking in the incinerator, the light fixtures, behind the stove and even checking the elevator shaft. They had found two guns, a target pistol and a rifle, but neither were semi-automatic.

Also, the .380 was a popular gun with both criminals and law-abiding citizens. The *FDNM* noted that it was small and carried a heavy punch, but with so many in circulation and no law requiring the registration of guns in Alaska, the newspaper already felt tracing the murder weapon was virtually impossible. Hunting and shooting were popular outdoor hobbies, and it was common for men, women and even children to own a gun. They were easily available, and no license was required.

Even so, neither the police record nor the FBI file mentions that law enforcement canvassed local pawn and gun shops to see if a .380 had been bought or sold recently. It should have been a routine part of the investigation, even if there was little chance of success.

Still, confidence was high, at least at the moment, though they did need to find the gun that killed Cecil.

At the well-attended council meeting held a few days after the murder, Danforth generally seemed to have the support of the public, and especially the Wells family. Reuben Tarte, who was administering Cecil's legal affairs, told the *FDNM* that they felt he was "doing a fine job," and had even offered funds to the police department if it was needed.

That opinion changed later, when the family shelled out money on celebrity sleuths and lawyers.

The *FDNM* also reported that council members weren't so concerned about what had been done at the beginning of the case, more about how it was managed from here on in. Several spoke both for and against Danforth, with everyone urging cooperation between the various agencies, and Fairbanks' Mayor even said they should "stop being prima donnas about it all."

Cecil's murder had started rumblings about the return of the Crime Squad, which Danforth had helped bring to an end, and in an attempt to clear the air and reassure the public, the *FDNM* urged cooperation, and featured a front-page article about Danforth and his investigation.

Quoted extensively in what very much sounded like an apologetic but belligerent tone, Danforth emphasized the importance of one agency being in control at first (i.e., his) so that nothing would be missed, duplicated or confused, and that he would have asked for help if he needed it. He also mentioned something that's always crucial in the early stages following a murder:

"That clock just keeps going around."

Taking careful note of the criticisms aimed at him during the council meeting, Danforth subsequently conferred with the Territorial Police, US Marshals, US Attorney's Office and other federal officers to discuss the leads in the case, and to formulate an overall plan. An arrest and prosecution was said to be "expected."

There was another small article on the front page that day: the details of Cecil's funeral. He lay in state, and there was going to be a viewing for the public and then the family before a 2.30pm ceremony at the Presbyterian Church, with Lloyd Martin, Jim Messer two of the pallbearers. His body was to be flown out of Fairbanks for the last time by private plane, with burial in Anchorage the following day. Diane and Marquam were there to pay their respects, among many others.

On page two, the effect that Cecil's murder had on the community was shown to have reached the pulpit of the local Lutheran Church. Their Reverend urged a probe of truth, and said that if the law agencies had been playing cat and mouse they deserved all the criticism, and that "laws are on the books to be enforced... in the interest of justice."

Catching Cecil's killer was going to be a big prize. Maybe not financially, but certainly personally, politically and even religiously. But who was going to win it?

As he banged the typewriter keys and vowed to prove his doubters wrong, Danforth concluded his report by writing that Cecil Wells could not have answered Diane when she nudged him, as he was already dead, and his parting shot was a very loud one.

"I believe Dianne (sic) Wells may be able to shed more light on this case."

In other words, he thought she was lying.

CHAPTER 8

The Photographs

Black and white but with a tinge of icy blue, the first crime scene photographs I received from the Alaska State Archives were close-ups of Cecil's body. The clearest one really did look like he was asleep, save for the large bloodstain that spread out like a puddle from his mouth onto the sheets and mattress under his head.

A fat stream of blood trickled down from the left side of his mouth, and there was a dark stain around the center of his ear. It looked like he had been killed just as his final words, or even a gasp of shock and pain, were leaving his body.

The fingers of his right hand were peeking out from under his left armpit, while other photographs taken from Diane's side of the bed showed his right arm drawn across his chest, somewhat like he was crossing his arms, though his left arm was rather awkwardly crooked, almost like a child making a lopsided teapot gesture. His left hand was almost covered in what looked like dried blood.

That he ended up in such an awkward position was probably due to rigor mortis, and the body settling after being hit by such an incredible force. The blanket was pulled down slightly below his waist level, perhaps because an officer wanted to make sure the bloody hand and the whole of Cecil's upper body would be captured on film.

Not included were close-up pictures of Cecil's bloodied head, and the fatal injury he had received. They would surely have been a priority at the time, but perhaps they had been considered too shocking to release into public archives? There were also no pictures of Diane and her injuries: that came on the front page of the *FDNM* a few days later.

The other photographs were less dramatic, though potentially held as many clues as the body in the bed.

Some of the drawers were slightly open on a grand chest of drawers, and there were some clothes on the floor, including Cecil's rifled trousers, but otherwise it seemed to indicate a pretty regular apartment. Even with some late-night packing for the Anchorage trip, nothing that looked like it had been ransacked.

However, one photograph shows an open briefcase balanced awkwardly on the arms of an armchair, and some boxes or maybe jewelry cases on the floor.

It seems like at least a cursory search of them was made, but maybe the thieves were interrupted or felt that they needed to make a run for it.

Other photographs showed packed closets, a telephone on the nest of tables, a large glass cabinet of doubtless expensive china, the portrait of Diane and Marquam on top of the radio cabinet where one of the flowerpots had been standing, a set of pans hanging on the kitchen wall, the bathrooms, and others. There were also photographs of the corridor outside and one looking down at the carpet, where there were some strange marks: bloodstains.

A couple more also really stood out.

One of them, taken after Cecil's body had been removed, shows the bed stripped of blankets, sheets, pillow cases and the mattress cover, some of which were sent to the FBI for analysis. Another showed the window nearby and its open curtains.

Then there was the fallen picture.

The picture, which seems to be of a woman with dark hair, usually hung from the connecting door that joined apartment 815 to 814. This door was said to be permanently closed, and Diane told the *FDNM* that the painting didn't hang on a nail, but from a strap that was jammed between the top of the door and the frame. So, if that door had been opened or pushed, the painting would have fallen down and landed in the armchair that was backed up against it.

Also in front of that armchair is a table that looks out of place, like it might have recently been moved there, perhaps by the fire/ambulance men or the investigating officers. A lot of people had been coming and going, and there wasn't much elbow room in their mid-sized apartment.

The photographs were potential evidence for a jury, but they didn't show any rulers or indicators of scale, nor any arrows or even pointing fingers to highlight things that were important. More than that, the descriptions on the back read like compass coordinates, often didn't list which apartment it was taken in, and weren't clearly sequential or comprehensive, something members of a jury, or other people who hadn't been to the crime scene, might well have found confusing.

There were also no close-up photographs of the evidence that was shipped to the FBI; the black women's shoes, the woolen cap, the bottles of alcohol with fingerprints on it, the blood on the pressure cooker button, the flowerpot that had been smashed over Diane's head, the blood stain on the carpet, the bullet they eventually found in the pillow, the soiled night clothes nor the replacement pajamas she had worn. There were also no photographs of the door's lock or safety chain (if there was one), which should have been taken to support or disprove Diane's account of a break-in.

It didn't seem like these photographs were missing, as a handwritten exhibits list in the coroner's file tallied with what had been sent, so I printed them out and constructed a patchwork-style pseudo-map of the living room and main bedroom.

The photographs of the kitchen, Marquam's bedroom and the doors of 814 and 815 were less revealing, and ultimately my pseudo-map didn't reveal any major clues. Many of the photographs were shot more medium/establishing than close-up, which didn't help with noting detail, but it did make sense: the photographer was on assignment from a portrait studio, and wasn't a law enforcement professional.

The photographs varied in size, from a very small, snapshot-style 3 x 2" to a larger 6 x 4 ½", but he may have been told to shoot and develop them that way, and who knows if photographs of closets full of dresses and coats might have meant something to a more trained eye? Even so, as a set of crime scene photographs, they really weren't that helpful. If nothing else, that they were black and white instead of color meant that bloodstains and dirt from the broken flowerpot would look very similar.

Other potential sources for photographs were a dead end. The Fisher Studio closed in the 1960s, and the *FDNM* tended to use freelance photographers, who kept the rights to their work. Even then, anything that might have been in the newspaper's office was probably destroyed in the enormous 1967 flood that hit the city.

Just in case, I again asked the Alaska State Archives if there were any other documents along with the crime scene photographs, and they sent details of an envelope they found that had the instructions "Hold for evidence Cecil Wells murder" written on the outside.

Inside it were a number of red, coral branch beads. No note and no explanation, just dozens of the beads, which the archivist kindly photographed alongside a quarter coin for reference. They were very small, and since they had holes in them it seemed they were probably from a necklace or bracelet. They seemed so innocuous, but they had been considered important enough to save. They didn't match any of the items that were allegedly stolen or recovered, so was Diane wearing this coral bracelet or necklace that night, and it got broken in the struggle with the intruder? If it was suspected there was blood or fingerprints on them they would have been sent to the FBI, but there was no mention of them anywhere else, and the archivist told me they had never been asked for.

So maybe they had got filed away, perhaps accidentally, and hadn't seen daylight for decades. Until now.

CHAPTER 9

Inquest No. 285

Fairbanks, Alaska - Tuesday October 20, 1953

Even though there was little question over what caused Cecil's death, the coroner's inquest into it was the longest in Fairbanks' history, and it started on a cloudy morning, October 20, at the Federal Building.

Built in the Art Deco style in 1933, its marble steps, terrazzo floors and bald eagle grillwork over the main doors are still impressive today. It was the third courthouse in this location, and also the home to the US Post Office. Sarah Crawford Isto wrote that many people had post office boxes because home delivery could be irregular, and collecting your mail was a chance to catch up on the local gossip.

The list of witnesses included virtually every person who had been at the Northward Building the morning of October 17, as well as Herb Mensing, newspaper photographer Jim Douthit, and others.

Described as still badly bruised and discolored, Diane took the stand, though before she even spoke her lawyer Walter Sczudlo said she and her friends were being intimidated, and that obvious attempts were being made to implicate her rather than trying to apprehend the two men.

Sczudlo, who also lived at the Northward in apartment 725 and whose wife had been interviewed as part of the investigation, advised her that since she had already given a statement to police, she should avoid incriminating herself and refuse to answer questions from Stevens and the US Territorial Commissioner.

The first real bombshell came when Cecil's fourth wife Ethel testified that he was "a jealous type of person," subject to fits of violence when he had been drinking. He had struck her "on numerous occasions" during their married life, even knocking her to the street in public, and once chased her and her mother around waving a pistol — though the strong-willed Ethel had often fought back, too.

Ethel was somewhat of an entrepreneur. Her son Wendell told me that she owned a gift shop in Fairbanks that imported figurines, jewelry, glassware, and fine china, high-end items you couldn't get unless you took a long flight or a steamship to the department stores of Seattle. She had also wanted to establish an idyllic "Santa Land" in North Pole, a real town some 14 miles outside Fairbanks, and got as far as persuading them to give her five acres of land before the plan ran out of money.

As the inquest dragged on, it became clear that the jury wasn't able to come to a conclusion about exactly what time Cecil had been killed. They had heard from the witnesses and been taken to see the Wells' apartment at the Northward, but still they wanted to know more.

Danforth had disagreed on the stand with Dr. McLean, who said that Cecil's hands were slightly colder than normal when he arrived, whereas Danforth said they were cold. Dr. McLean hadn't taken Cecil's liver or rectal temperature, though the comparison of that to the environmental temperature as way to help determine time of death wasn't common practice at the time.

It might not have mattered anyway, because Danforth also disagreed with Dr. Haggland's verdict that fixed the time of death as around five hours before the police arrived. Despite his lack of medical training, he insisted that Cecil died shortly before Diane called for help.

His conduct on the stand wasn't helping, and he visibly bristled when DA Stevens asked him about the "conduct" of the investigation. It was a valid question, as the laboratory technician at the Fairbanks Medical and Surgical Clinic had blamed inadequate equipment for the negative result on the blood samples that Danforth had ordered before sending them to the FBI.

There was no such thing as DNA profiling in 1953, but the public understood that blood came in various types, and that a sample of blood collected from a crime scene could be linked to someone who shared that same group, though that didn't necessarily make them guilty of anything.

What if the person whose blood was on the tested shoes and/or the pressure cooker button had gone on the run? Getting a flight out of Fairbanks wouldn't have been a problem, but getting suspects back from the Lower 48 always involved red-tape and the need to justify the expense of extraditing the suspect (and maybe an escort) back. The delay had only been a short one, but every minute counts in the immediate aftermath of a killing.

It also wasn't the only problem with the crime scene forensics.

During the inquest, Officer Thrift admitted that he couldn't take accurate fingerprints off the liquor bottles because they were "smeared." Fairbanks didn't have the resources for specialist forensics officers, let alone the equipment to analyze the results, and while everyone in law enforcement understood this, to the jury and those sitting in the public gallery, it didn't sound very professional. The fingerprint samples in the FBI file looked fairly clear, at least to my untrained eye.

But appearances can be deceptive, and smeared or not, these fingerprints were later compared to many others.

Danforth also reserved some choice words for Diane. He rejected the notion that she was hysterical or crying, saying she was simply agitated, and added that she smelled of alcohol. He also said that she willingly went to hospital, rather than insisting Cecil went first, and scored a point when his claim that she had no dirt or foreign matter on her from the African violets and earth in the flowerpot was backed up by two nurses from St. Joseph's.

Danforth now went on the record dismissing any talk of a robbery.

The apartment was barely disturbed, he said, adding that he felt Cecil was shot from the north side of the bed that Diane slept in, just as Haggland said in his autopsy report, though Diane said the intruder shot Cecil from the opposite south side.

Following an early adjournment but no verdict, the jury asked for a continuance so they could hear from more witnesses and read pathology reports. One of the jury members, assistant postmaster Joe Simpson, also seemed to have questions, because included in the coroner's report file was a page on his USPS letterhead. It was hand-dated October 28 and notably featured the word "pajamas" among some brief notes. He had stood and asked Diane directly if she was shielding anyone, or knew who the assailants were.

She shook her head in reply.

To complicate matters further, the inquest was running at the same time as Fairbanks' annual grand jury was convened at the federal building. An often-controversial quirk of the legal system, in part because only the prosecutor is allowed to present evidence, their randomly-selected 23 jurors would be hearing cases ranging from larceny to perjury to murder, in secret, over a three-to-four-week period.

Despite working very long hours, they routinely failed to deal with all the cases on the docket — some 100 in 1953 — and the inevitable logjam could see some dismissed or not even raised, so DA Stevens was desperate to get the Wells case added to the list while they were still in session.

The coroner's inquest continued though. Herb Mensing, the Wells' dinner guest, had flown in especially but had little to add besides saying the pair seemed in a "happy and compatible" mood that night, while Kathleen Walker, who lived on the floor below the Wells, said she had been up until around 4am making hats, but "did not hear one sound" from above.

Before she went to bed though, she heard the sound of two men running down the stairway from the eighth floor. The door to the staircase was directly opposite her front door, and one of them said: "Oh no, no" while the other grumbled something in return. Frightened, she locked her door and heard the two men take the elevator.

Who were they? Late night-partyers, or the two attackers running from the crime scene?

The next day Walker's testimony added that the two men she heard could have come up from the sixth floor as well as down from the eighth, something a sharp lawyer would certainly have pointed out in a trial.

As the inquest finally drew to a close, it seemed inevitable that the last witness would be Diane, who was making her third appearance on the stand. Still with a bruised face, she was "obviously emotionally upset" and reportedly on the verge of tears at some of Stevens' questions. She agreed to his question about taking a lie detector test, and told the jury that she had never heard anyone threaten her husband's life.

The jury began its final deliberations while Danforth was waiting anxiously for the FBI findings, which they received via air mail in a brief, all-caps summary on October 28, the same day a curious crowd of nearly 200 squeezed into the courtroom to hear the verdict. Shivering as the temperature hovered around zero, more people outside had already been turned away.

They ruled that "the deceased came to his death by means of a bullet shot from a .380 caliber gun," and that the wound was "inflicted by persons or persons unknown between the hours of two and four o'clock in the morning."

They also made four recommendations, the first of which was to proceed with the lie detector test Diane volunteered to take, though the other three were related to local law enforcement.

Firstly, that all agencies should be called in on felony cases; secondly that no one agency should assume sole responsibility of accumulating evidence; and thirdly that the coroner should be called immediately in the case of an unnatural death before major evidence is destroyed, lost or removed. They urged the agencies to work together, so that the person or persons responsible would be brought to justice.

It was an inspiring tone with which to finish their duty, but those recommendations felt like more rebukes aimed squarely at Danforth, who was already hearing rumors about people calling for his resignation or outright firing.

Diane continued to be questioned after the inquest, and a few days later Cecil's murder was added to the grand jury docket — probably on top of the pile — with Stevens' recommendation that charges should be brought against Diane. Even without the neighbor's reports of arguments in the Wells household, or the fact that Cecil was the wealthy, older husband, her unconvincing story about the robbery had been enough to turn her from a victim to a suspect.

Also, unknown to the public at the time, there were some private letters that the police had in their possession barely a week after the murder.

To ensure the chain of evidence, the four love letters had been initialed by EVD (E.V. Danforth) and others alongside the date they received them: October 25, 1953.

One undated card has a cute bunny design with slogan alongside "Been thinking LOTS of you today!", while handwritten underneath is: "I haven't gone yet, but I miss you already — a kiss for you." It was signed "AC".

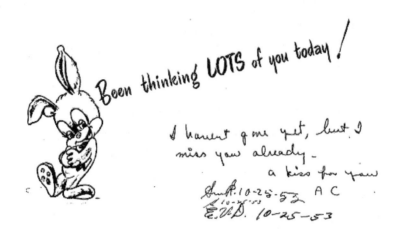

Another is postmarked Seattle on September 28, 1953, and was addressed to Johnny at the Piggly Wiggly in Fairbanks, as she obviously couldn't send letters to his marital home.

Inside was a small Norcross greeting card, and on it was a handwritten poem:

There was a girl who loved a boy,
but she was could never quite say the
serious things she felt about him, until
one day when they were together she said -
"I long to tell you how I feel,
But somehow I just dread it,'
but the impulse sort of took her over
and she just sort of let it,
and when she told him of her love
She sighed 'at least I said it.'"
He looked at her and then replied
I think you must have read it.

The word "read" was underlined several times.

A second letter was postmarked Seattle on September 29, and also sent to the Piggly Wiggly. Addressed to "Darling," it says that "I'm a happy girl now, just picked up your letter. It's very hard for me to get away."

It refers to an unsuccessful attempt to talk by phone, and the fact that he had apparently saw her off at the airport. "I wished you had stayed a little longer… maybe sat across from us after we left the coffee shop — just so I could have seen you a little longer. I suppose you know me, though, I'd have given myself away."

This sounded like risky behavior between lovers — catching each other's eye while the husband was there — but perhaps Diane had been taking Marquam down to Seattle? It was commonplace for people to visit that city, which had many more department stores and attractions than Fairbanks or Anchorage, and she signs off:

"Heard you have snow. It's raining down here. Sunny in my heart though, because of you."

Another undated, unaddressed card with a flower design has a sentimental motto that ends with a line about "Our "get-together" day" and the handwritten words "look inside." It also has the words "P.S. Alice Colby in case you've forgotten," scribbled on it. This could be the "AC" of the other letter,

53

and when I couldn't find any strong connection to that name in the archives I wondered if this was a code or a secret name?

On the reverse of the card is a chatty summary of a trip to a 700-guest wedding in Seattle, which was also attended by the Martins. Diane also mentions she hadn't had time to go to the post office, which seems to show that the person she was writing to was replying to her letters. In those days of course, a phone call to Alaska would have been expensive.

That said, this could simply be a florid, romantic letter Diane wrote to Cecil. The language doesn't seem to ring true though, especially since it ends with "...how very much I miss you," a promise to "call that number you gave me," and "I love you darling, and wish you were here with me. Yours always," with a small heart alongside the letter "D".

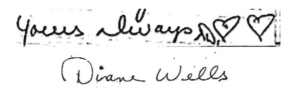

That sign-off symbol "D" and a heart was immediately recognizable. The September 29 letter seemed to have a tiny version of it too, but more memorably, it appeared on another note from Diane some six months later.

There is also a partly-torn, undated page taken from a letter that Diane seemed to have written to Cecil. In it she talks about a stain on the carpet, taking hula lessons, and how Marq likes nursery school and wants a car, not a tricycle, and that she will get him one from "the garage" (surely meaning Cecil's dealership). But then she writes about Marquam:

"He says you're in Hawaii when anybody asks him."

Was Cecil actually somewhere else, and Marquam had been told to keep it a secret? There was no explanation for this.

Also dated October 25 by law enforcement was a writing sample that has Diane's signature at the top and bottom and reads:

I have been away so long the weather is nice I'll see you soon again hope your (sic) well.

The murder charges had been issued by the time this sample and the love letters were sent to the FBI, but now the investigation was looking to prove that they were lovers and possible co-conspirators.

On December 19, a Laboratory Work Sheet came back from the FBI with the results of another handwriting sample Diane had provided. The lines made no sense, but featured key words to the investigation.

Johnny Warren Fairbanks
I haven't yet but your kiss for
Darling picked just it's had wish I your
I gave to your left for have D of (unreadable)
I think you must said (unreadable)
from when get asks about the Diane is

A number of small arrows showed the analyst had concluded the writing samples matched, and though graphology or handwriting analysis is often dismissed today, this connection between Diane and Johnny would certainly have been used in a trial.

It was another piece of evidence that led to Stevens also recommending that Johnny Warren was charged as her co-conspirator. It was an unexpected reversal, as the previous day's *FDNM* had reported that there were no "hot" suspects, and that since there was only circumstantial evidence against Johnny, no indictment was expected against him.

However, in San Francisco, California, Johnny had already been talking to the police, which was probably when he handed them the love letters, or told them where they could be found.

CHAPTER 10

Johnny Talks

San Francisco, California — Tuesday October 27, 1953

Johnny's long, multi-day drive had ended when he arrived at his sister Willia's house in the San Antonio district of Oakland, California, and the week or so he spent there were the last peaceful days he had for many years.

The "calm but uncommunicative" Johnny was voluntarily taken from Willia's home by Inspector James Mangini and a San Francisco US Marshal. He spent barely a day in Alameda County jail, some 25 or so miles outside Oakland, before being moved to the San Francisco County jail at the Hall of Justice.

As the temperature dipped into the fifties, around 10.30pm on October 27 he was brought into room 203, and started talking to Mangini and fellow inspector Don Ainsworth. He said he'd return to Fairbanks immediately if someone would pay his way, and volunteered for a lie detector test. That test proved to be inconclusive, but officials said that was probably because the operator didn't know enough about the case to question him adequately.

Reports said that the conversation between Johnny, Mangini, and Ainsworth lasted for anything between nine to 19 hours, and that his statement was over 20 pages long. He wasn't under arrest, not at that stage, and though I wasn't able to obtain a copy of the actual statement, many extracts were reported in the newspapers.

Mangini quickly brought up the fact that Diane was white and he was "colored." As an African-American man who had allegedly been having an affair with the (white) wife of a successful (white) businessman who had been

57

found murdered, it always seemed certain — at least to me — that no matter what happened, Johnny was definitely going to end up in prison.

More than that, Johnny was himself married. His wife's name was Clara, and not only was she pregnant, she was also white, and, according to the *Indianapolis Recorder*, worked as accountant at one of Cecil's companies.

The press talked to Clara, who told the *San Francisco Call-Bulletin* that "I know Johnny is innocent. I'm positive of it. I'm certainly going to stick by him." Whether she had read Johnny's statement by this stage isn't known, so perhaps it was Willia who suggested he go willingly with the police, and get his story on the record.

Tall and handsome with a pencil mustache and a rather rakish smile, Johnny admitted in the interview that Diane had first made advances to him at the Fairbanks Country Club Labor Day event ("advances" was the word Mangini used). According to the *El Paso Herald-Post*, Johnny had been glancing out on the dance floor when Diane caught his eye.

"I thought she winked at me," he said, and when she did it again, he was sure of it. "She kept looking at me, and sorta smiling over Mr. Wells' shoulder." He smiled back, confident now that these "advances with her eyes" meant that "she might appreciate attention."

A couple of days later Johnny called her from the Piggly Wiggly, and coyly refused to identify himself at first, probably to make sure that Diane was alone and could talk. For a few minutes they flirtily played a guessing game of "who am I?", but once she identified the mystery caller, instead of asking him what he wanted, Diane told Johnny that he had "disappointed" her.

The telephone to-and-fro continued, as Johnny asked what he had done to upset her. Diane said that she had seen him in another club a couple of years ago, and was interested in him because of what he had been doing: yawning at the burlesque act. Rather boastfully, Johnny said that "she was fascinated by a man who could be so disinterested while a young woman was undressing in front of him."

She had "inquired" about him at that time, but decided to forget about it when she learned he was married.

In the two years since, something had presumably changed for Diane —

perhaps in her marriage — and while Johnny said she was always with somebody else (presumably Cecil), he had noticed her a few times at the Fairbanks Country Club recently, and she had made those advances to him several times. He would have been surprised and flattered to learn that the most attractive woman in town had him in her sights for so long, and that surely enhanced the thrill of the chase.

After they had talked on the phone for a while, Diane asked him if he would like to come up to the apartment for a drink. Her offer was a challenge, as it might be the moment when something could happen between them. It was also a moment of decision for Johnny, who asked her if it was "safe," as he knew that she was married. When she said that it was, he went up that afternoon and had several drinks with her.

Daringly, Diane called Johnny at work the next day and asked if he wanted to visit again that afternoon. He did, but a few minutes after arriving, Diane said that she was feeling uneasy: did he know another place where they could go? Fairbanks was a small city, and while they might have exchanged polite words at a busy club night, two married people meeting in public would have been noticed, and neither could risk (another) liaison in their marital homes, or being seen at a local hotel. It was another romantic challenge, but emotions must have been running high between them because Johnny immediately called his friend and fellow musician Kenny Wadsworth, who offered up his apartment in the nearby Polaris Building. However, Diane now said that she would only go there on one condition: that his friend wouldn't be there; she didn't want anyone to see them together.

Johnny hurried the couple of blocks to the Polaris, and persuaded the understanding Wadsworth to make himself scarce. Johnny said that he and Diane met in the Polaris "quite a few times" after that, and also in the stairwell of the Northward, a scenario that seemed to suggest an intense and even reckless passion grew quickly between them. Maybe Diane had again been swept up in a romantic whirlwind.

So there it was. Albeit in a rather roundabout way, Johnny had formally admitted there had been "intimate relations" between him and Diane.

Johnny Warren Tells of Trysts

In other parts of the extensive interview, Johnny said that Diane had expressed the feeling she was "not contented" in her marriage, and that she had no objection to the racial differences between them being a possible barrier to their seeking divorces and marrying one another.

Perhaps this was just fanciful pillow talk, as Johnny later told the detectives that he was not in love with Diane, and it would be "hard to answer" if she were in love with him. It might have been more of a physical attraction at the beginning, but things had obviously changed — at least for Diane.

It's worth remembering that this was Johnny's side of the story, and that he was speaking as a man who had become connected to a notorious murder. He might have been trying to protect himself by distancing himself from Diane, and added later in the interview that they never discussed doing away with Cecil, and that he didn't know if she had anything to do with his death.

As for the last time he saw her, he said that was on October 15, when he told her he was going to Oakland because he was "having trouble" with his wife. Diane told him not to go, and perhaps this was the stairwell meeting; a tense conversation between soon-to-be-separated lovers.

The night of the murder, he went to work at the Fairbanks Country Club and got a phone call there around 9.30pm. It was a man who had heard he was going to Oakland, and asked if he would he take a paying passenger? Johnny agreed, and the potential passenger said he would meet him in the Northward lobby between 2 and 4am.

After finishing work at the club around 1.30am, Johnny drove Wadsworth to a restaurant and dropped off another friend before going home to pack. Around 2.30am he drove to the Northward, but aside from a man in a white coat who Johnny thought might be a butcher or a baker about to go to work, it seemed that his paying ride had changed his mind.

Johnny got going, as he had already had two other passengers: Betty Craig, an African-American family friend who wanted to be dropped off in Seattle, and he and Clara's recently-adopted daughter Susanna. He made a makeshift bed for Susanna in the back of his car, a Pontiac Sedan that the newspaper deliberately mentioned he had bought from Cecil's dealership (the only one in town), and the trio started their late-night drive to the Outside.

One of the vital things Mangini and Ainsworth needed to know was whether Johnny owned a gun, and if he carried it on his person. Johnny frankly admitted that he had three guns while he was in Fairbanks: a .38 special, an 8mm semi-automatic Italian Beretta, and a "cheap" Cain gun which had two barrels, the one on top being a .32, the bottom being a .44.

The inspectors knew about one of them already; they had found the .38, a nickel-colored Colt, in his luggage, and Johnny confirmed it was the same gun. As for the "antique" gun (presumably the Cain), Johnny said he left that with Clara, while he had sold the 8mm to a "stranger" for $10 in the washroom of the Talk of The Town about two weeks earlier. Johnny described this stranger as white, very tall, about 25 years old, 190 pounds, heavy set with a thin face, clean shaven, wearing glasses and seemed to be blond. He was also wearing a hat.

Johnny freely admitted carrying weapons "on several occasions" while in Fairbanks, and seemed to imply that this included when he would meet Diane at the Northward: he "felt better coming up there and having the gun in case anything would happen." He was pressed on what this meant, and admitted that he would have used the gun to protect himself "if Mr. Wells surprised him."

There's so much detail in Johnny's statement that it's hard to dismiss it as fiction. Diane had strongly denied the relationship, and was even quoted as saying she "didn't know him from Adam." If it became a he said, she said, he may have rightly feared that the odds wouldn't be in his favor.

Either way, the many pages of his statement could be boiled down to one sentence: he and Diane had been having an affair; he was at the Northward close to the time Cecil was murdered; and he had been carrying a gun.

It was an unfortunate coincidence at best, and downright incriminating at worst.

CHAPTER 11

Arrested for Murder

Seattle, Washington / Oakland, California — November 3-6, 1953

No. 177 Cr.

I N D I C T M E N T

The Grand Jury charges in this Indictment:

That Johnny Warren and Diana Wells, on the 17th day of October, 1953,

in the Fourth Division, Territory of Alaska, then and there being and being of

sound memory and discretion, did feloniously, purposely and of deliberate and

premeditated malice, kill another, to-wit, Cecil Wells, a human being, by shoot-

ing him, the said Cecil Wells, with a pistol, in violation of Section 65-4-1

of the Alaska Compiled Laws Annotated, 1949.

DATED at Fairbanks, Alaska, this 3rd day of November, 1953.

The docket page was much starker than the indictment. Under the names
of the accused it simply read:

CRIME: First Degree Murder

The arrest orders had been issued in secret on November 3, but by the
time Stevens had signed them and they had been issued, Diane had left for
Seattle en route to Los Angeles.

Maybe the declaration that there were no "hot" suspects had been a tactic to stop her leaving Fairbanks, but now both she and Johnny were out of the territory, the US Marshals and the police forces in the Lower 48 came to the forefront, and Danforth must have been furious.

Reporters and photographers were waiting for Diane and Marquam when they arrived in Seattle, and, wearing a fur coat and carrying a mink cape, she was immediately arrested around 9.15pm by a US Marshal and two members of local law enforcement. The *Seattle Times* reported that she wept as they escorted her off the plane, and while she must have suspected she was going to be charged with the murder of her husband, it was surely a sobering moment when she found the three lawmen waiting for her.

Distressed and confused, she was taken to King County Jail to hear the charges against her. Marquam seemed unaffected by all the fuss, and the *Daily Sitka Sentinel* said he played noisily and happily at the jail house and then stayed with Diane's lawyer, Walter Sczudlo, while she was temporarily behind bars.

The *San Francisco Chronicle* quoted Diane as saying she had been through a brain washing, and that she had "been awake for so many hours I don't know what I said," but as the enormity of the situation became clear to her, she began to defend herself.

Later she was described as fighting mad, denied Johnny's claim that they were "very friendly," and told the *New York Journal-American* she was "determined to clear my name and my son's name," and that "It seems the only way I'll be able to do it is to find my husband's killer and that is what I intend to do, so help me!… if it takes the rest of my life."

They were brave words, and displaying a surprising confidence she waived extradition and, on a $5,000 bond, flew back to Fairbanks on the midnight plane with Marquam and Sczudlo — but no official escort — a couple of days later. There was a shot of her in the *Los Angeles Times* "posing for photographers in Seattle," and she was also photographed by the *FDNM* getting off the plane at 6am, light snow falling as Marquam was carried off by a helpful passenger.

Coincidentally or not, the photographs always made her look like the classic femme fatale, her platinum blonde hair and white face dominating the dark mourning clothes she was wearing, with some of them even suggesting she was running from the flashbulbs and fighting her way through a crowd clamoring to ask "Did you kill him?" and "Where's Johnny?" No wonder she was quoted in the *FDNM* as having been "snowed under" with long-distance calls from newspapers as far away as London, England, in the wake of her arrest.

Asked if she felt the local townspeople were "down on her," she replied "No, not except for this other element," by which she meant Johnny's statement. She also told reporters that Johnny had not been at the apartment on the night of the murder, something that seemed to some like an admission that he had been there at another time.

The temperature that early morning was a biting seven degrees below zero, and the exhausted mother and son were quickly whisked away by Sczudlo to the Northward, though she and Marquam weren't going home; they stayed in a "smaller" apartment, where they were apparently in seclusion.

Oakland Drummer Held
JAZZ MAN, WIDOW SEIZED IN MURDER

Johnny had been arrested on November 5, but the Oakland Police wouldn't hold him indefinitely, and he made it clear he wanted to fight extradition to Fairbanks because there was a "wave of prejudice" against him there. Whether he meant racial prejudice is not known for sure, but he and his brother surely had some bad memories of their time in the segregated US Army during WWII.

Territorial Alaska was actually at the forefront regarding race issues, as it had passed the Equal Rights Act in 1945.

Admittedly it applied more to their large, previously-segregated and restricted Alaskan Native population rather than the tiny African-American one, but it did lead to the end of Jim Crow laws in the territory — though of course that in no way meant that prejudice had disappeared overnight, especially in these circumstances.

The 1950 census, which Johnny and his wife Clara would have been part of, showed that Alaska was 72% white, 26% "Aleut/Eskimo/Indian", and 2% "Other", while 2019 figures show that Asian and Latinos are now ahead of the African-American population too.

Had Diane's lover been white, he would have undoubtedly come under suspicion and been questioned too. He might even have been charged alongside her, given the same circumstances, though the investigative manner of the case would certainly have been different, at least in terms of the approach and attitude of law enforcement.

Johnny's African-American lawyer John W. Bussey argued whether extradition between a state and a territory was the same as between states, but after a couple of weeks the extradition went ahead. Johnny then asked Everett Hepp, his lawyer in Fairbanks, to argue for a separate trial from Diane.

If he was found guilty of Cecil's murder, there was the remote possibility he might face the death penalty.

Often a jury would qualify its verdict "without capital punishment", which instead meant a lifetime of hard labor in prison, and since 1900 Alaska had only legally executed eight men (and no women). However, that number included three in Fairbanks (two Native non-English speakers in 1921 and 1929, and a Montenegrin from Europe, also in 1921).

More alarmingly, two African-Americans, Austin Nelson and Eugene LaMoore, had been hung in Juneau in 1948 and 1950 respectively for the robbing and violent killing of a white storekeeper. Their convictions were controversial, and the circumstances — one man pulled the trigger, but both were charged with murder — were uncomfortably close to those of the Cecil Wells murder case.

Within days of the arrests, the photograph from the night when Johnny and Diane allegedly "met" for the first time had hit the newspapers.

September 5, 1953 had been a mild night, and was just another Saturday gig at the Fairbanks Country Club.

The Johnny Warren Orchestra had been playing there since it opened for the season a few months before, but tonight a number of politicians, including congressman E.L. "Bob" Bartlett, were going to be celebrating the upcoming Labor Day, and that was why Jim Douthit took a soon-to-be-notorious photograph of the evening's entertainment.

It showed an opulent dining room with well-dressed guests eating and drinking while Warren's band played on stage in the background. The musicians were dressed just as handsomely, but were different from everyone else in the photograph: they all seemed to be African-American.

Now with helpful arrows added, readers could easily see Diane's smiling face and blond hair on the left (looking like it might have been touched-up to stand out more), while indicated on the right was a distracted-looking Johnny playing the drums.

It was evidence of nothing besides their attendance, but in the wake of Cecil's murder the *Los Angeles Herald-Express* splashed the headline "Millionaire Widow Denies Love Tryst," and below the photograph wrote "The Millionaire, The Blonde Wife and the Drummer."

A few days later, *Newsweek* printed the photograph and asked: "Did a wink and a phone call lead to murder?".

An irresistible call for lovers of scandal, this photograph ran across the country, and arguably had the greatest effect on public opinion about the murder, and particularly who was the guilty party.

NeverLuredJazz Drummer With Eyes, SaysBlonde

An angry Diane had immediately hit back, and told reporters she "never flirted with anyone in my life, especially a man like him." It was a quote that seems laced with racism, but it reflected the attitudes and morals of the time

— and as letters would later show, it was also a lie.

In the rush to leave the airport at Fairbanks, Diane had left her luggage behind. This reminded me of something that Byron Halvorson said: that when Diane first went to jail, he went with Diane's attorney Wallace Aiken to collect some of her suitcases.

"We went through them, looking for incriminating evidence," admitted Byron. "But there was nothing there, just girls' stuff, ladies' stuff."

Whether they had collected her forgotten luggage or it was at another time, it sounded like they were prepared to remove or hide something that could have been important to the investigation. The fact that Aiken risked his career, and the potential arrest of both him and Byron, was starkly revealing in terms of what he thought about his new client.

CHAPTER 12

Diana/Diane

During her short life she was called Dissie, Diana, Shelley, Barbara and Doris, but Diane's story really began long before she was born — and so did her connection to Fairbanks.

Her mother Florence Dorothy was born in Missoula, Montana on September 18, 1897 to Zoe and Andrew Burdick, and was the eldest of their four children. Florence seemed to have an unsettled childhood, because around 1900 she became a ward of physicians Charles and Sarah Hill of Portland, Oregon.

I never found any documents confirming whether Florence was formally adopted, but the young toddler was the newest member of a very wealthy and influential family; Sarah was the daughter of Philip Augustus Marquam, a lawyer, judge and the largest landowner in Multnomah County.

There's still a Marquam Gulch, Marquam Nature Park, and Marquam Bridge across the Willamette River, but perhaps best known is Marquam Hill, which is better known as "Pill Hill" because of the hospitals and Oregon's Health & Science University that are located there. There's also an unincorporated community of Marquam in Clackamas County.

According to *Good Time Girls of the Alaska-Yukon Gold Rush*, Philip fathered 11 children including Sarah and Thomas, who was their youngest son. Thomas caught gold fever and headed up to Alaska in the late 1800s, and ending up living with his family in Fairbanks and practicing as a lawyer, where his life and career was a colorful and controversial one.

Known as "Fighting Tom" for his courtroom style and arrests for street brawls, he was popular among the locals for defending prostitutes, gamblers and bar owners, many of whom he enjoyed the company of outside office hours.

Like his grand-niece Diane he faced public scandal over an affair, though the charges brought against him were actually similar to those Cecil and Maud faced — only Thomas was found not guilty.

In 1923 he was elected Mayor of Fairbanks, during which time he persuaded President Warren G. Harding to visit and drive home the final golden spike of the railway that linked Fairbanks to the port of Seward. Whispers of an affair and a charge of election fraud scuppered any further political ambitions, though when Thomas died aged 57 in 1931, rumors of suicide and murder swirled in the air.

Diane's father was Charles Dean Baker, a railway clerk born in Colorado on May 29, 1898, and he and Florence were married on Feb 12, 1920 in Portland, Oregon. Since his father's name was also Charles he was called "Harry" by the family, and they welcomed their only child on Sunday January 15, 1922.

The baby was christened Dissie Diana (not Diane), the name Dissie apparently a nickname of Sarah Hill, though it seems her parents' marriage only lasted a few years, and that Diane barely had a relationship with her father. Florence took Diane to San Francisco around 1926, which might have been a fresh start after the break-up, and soon after that she began calling herself Yvonne both professionally and personally — though Florence will be used here.

Florence's great-granddaughter London had done a great deal of research on her, and bought two ceramic plates that she had created. Titled "Cable Cars on California Street," they featured colorful, almost caricature, representations of the famous San Francisco cable cars traveling through Chinatown, and were signed with a swirly "Yvonne." A number of her other San Francisco-centric works have been available for purchase online too.

I learned later that Diane had taken ceramics classes in Fairbanks. In a 2004 interview her teacher recalled that she was "talented and artistic," and I wondered whether Diane's mother had shared her skills with her.

Being a single mother was a challenge for Florence, and perhaps an accident, illness or another life event complicated her day-to-day life even further, because when Diane was around six years old, Florence sent her to an orphanage. An archive log book shows Diane — and she was Diane now, as Dissie was in parentheses — was admitted to the Maria Kip Orphanage on November 3, 1928, and discharged on June 14, 1930.

MARIA KIP ORPHANAGE
REPORT OF ADMISSIONS AND DISCHARGES
ADMITTED

Date	Name	By whom admitted
1928 Nov 3	(Dissie) Diana Baxer	Her mother

DISCHARGED

Date	Name	By whom taken
1930 June 8	Alpha Connor	Her mother
June 17	May Willson	" aunt
June 14	Diana Baxer	" Mother

Despite the name, some orphanages acted like day care or boarding school facilities at the time, but the archivist for the Episcopal Diocese of California told me frankly that Diane would have been a resident "24/7", and that in addition to orphans they took in children who the parent or parents could not care for, for whatever reason.

This meant that both mother and daughter spent time as wards, away from their parents. Florence's experience seemed to be a happy one, but it was hard to know what effect nearly 18 months in institutional care might have had on eight-year-old Diane. Did Florence write and visit, or did Diane spend that time wondering if she was ever going to see her mother again?

CHAPTER 13

Broken Sweethearts

Diane moved into the adult world (and out of her mother's home) almost as soon as possible.

On Saturday October 1, 1938, at Pacific Grove in Monterey, California, the 16-year-old Diane married 17-year-old Donald Henry Walker, an insurance salesman, garage mechanic and Ace Hardware clerk, who was born in Idaho on May 7, 1921. Their love must have been very powerful, because apparently Donald sued his mother in court so they could apply for a marriage license as they were both underage.

Florence must have supported the young lovers, as she was a witness at the wedding, though strangely she signed her name as Florence Ward on the wedding certificate, rather than her married name of Baker. She and Diane's father Charles had separated, and I couldn't find any evidence of her marrying a man named Ward. Even when she remarried in 1951, and for years afterward, she used the last name Ward.

Diane and Donald were said to have met at Pacific Grove High School, but only Donald's photograph was in the yearbooks, and the school had no record of Diane as a student. Perhaps this was just a romantic story they liked to tell, as family legend said that they in fact met when Diane came out to spend the summer vacation with her mother in Monterey, which is about 120 miles south of San Francisco.

During the first week of their marriage, their beach front cottage burned to the ground because Diane left the waffle iron plugged in when they left the house. The only things that were saved were Diane's wedding dress and his blue, pin-striped wedding suit.

They then moved to Grass Valley, part of Sacramento, and just over a year later they become parents when Saundra Diane was born on Tuesday November 7, 1939. That middle name choice of "Diane" instead of Diana was significant, as it showed she had truly left her childhood behind her.

An article in the *Auburn Journal* a couple of days later reported that Sarah Hill had visited Diane and Donald to see her "new great granddaughter," which seems to show that Diane's mother Florence had been officially adopted at some time after all. Whether that was the case or not, it made me wonder about the time Diane spent at the Maria Kip orphanage: surely Florence would have asked the Hills for help?

Then again, maybe she didn't want to let her parents know that she was struggling in her independent life. Perhaps Florence felt there had to be some bending of the truth, and even some sacrifices, to give her and her daughter the life they deserved.

In 1940 Diane's estranged father Harry, who had remarried and fathered two more children (Diane's half-siblings), died at the age of 42, and then in 1941 the spirit of adventure seemed to bewitch the young newlyweds. Donald and a friend decided to go to Alaska and work in construction, and, according to family legend, Diane went to Hollywood to try her luck in the movies.

The idea that Diane had gone to Hollywood was a tantalizing one, especially when it was rumored that she had got in with the wrong crowd and been arrested, but there was no record of her with the LAPD; no stylish mugshot. Florence had apparently performed in vaudeville as a dancer, but there was no record of that, either.

Whatever Diane was doing in Hollywood, it was a confusing near-abandonment for the infant Saundra:

"I do not know who I lived with then. My dad was in Alaska. I do not know who was taking care of me, and that's frightening."

Diane didn't return until Saundra says she was around two years old, and her father Donald came back home after witnessing the Battle of Dutch Harbor, a Japanese two-day air bombing raid on Alaska in June 1942 that saw dozens of deaths and injuries. Donald and his friend hadn't struck it rich anyway, and "his story was that he needed that money because Diane wanted a certain lifestyle."

He collected Diane and Saundra, and the reunited family went up to Washington state, where they and some friends built them a cabin at Hood Canal, an area in Puget Sound where the Hills, Diane's adoptive grandparents, spent their summers. It was a time Saundra looked back with mainly fond memories.

"When it was being built we camped out, and I remember the hammock that I was in. It would frequently turn over and dump me out. And I remember the berries we would eat. They just grew wild. And I remember an adult making pancakes over a grill made out of rock or something. In the magical forest. And I loved that as a kid. I would just take off by myself. I'd take my BB gun. And I'd go hunt. And in the winter when there were footsteps in the snow, I would track them."

She added quietly: "My parents were obviously in love when they married," while earlier that day, London told me that Saundra "wants justice for Diane."

Another happy memory for Saundra was when she accompanied her mother to the studio of English-born artist Waldo Chase, who had dark brown hair and a big, bushy mustache, and she showed me a photo of this studio. Born in Seattle on March 7, 1895, Chase was a self-taught printmaker and woodcutter who was noted for images and landscapes of the Pacific Northwest, especially Washington State.

"I would play with brushes and paint and stuff. He let me paint. My mother painted, too. We were happy there. The other place she took me was the bar. I didn't like it, but people were nice."

Her younger sister Bonnie June Walker was born just outside Seattle on Monday June 29, 1943, and I casually asked Saundra what Diane was like as a mother.

"She did not bring me up. She dropped me off at kindergarten one day, and then I never saw her again. I must have been about five. I didn't know what happened to her or where she went, because no one would tell me. My sister didn't know Diane at all because she was too young."

Diane never called or wrote, and Saundra said she thought that her mother had disappeared into thin air.

"I do remember my mom just a little bit. But I don't remember any closeness or tenderness. All I remember is that it was my job to take care of Bonnie."

Saundra rarely used the term mom or mother, nearly always calling her "Diane", but this was still a revelation. Had Diane abandoned her daughters?

Her father never spoke about it and Saundra never questioned it, in part, it seemed, out of fear of him. Donald was plagued by asthma as a child, and it seemed he had a very tough childhood at the hands of his own father. He too became a strict disciplinarian, and struggled to bring up the two girls. At the time he covered a large territory as a highway patrolman, and once had to kill a man who had slashed two bar patrons with a broken bottle, and then attacked him.

"My dad just couldn't handle it. He had a paddy wagon that he would put me in the back of, and I was terrified of it. He had wanted a boy, and he challenged me to do boy things. Like he'd put me on the roof, stand underneath, and tell me to jump. And I wouldn't do it. So then I was called a 'sissy'."

She also remembers when he bought her a BB gun:

"He taught me to shoot it. Shoot cans off the fence. Stuff like that. He struggled for about a year and then we were whisked away to his parents (Bill and Leona "Lee") in Ogden, Utah. We became Mormons. Being a Mormon means you have one hundred percent attendance at church. You're a better person than anybody you know. Perfection is the name of the game. You don't smoke, you don't drink, you don't pet. You don't do anything until you're married. I held fast with all of that."

Saundra told me that Diane later denied even having children, and I asked if she thought Diane had left the family to be with another man. Saundra said she knew for a fact that Diane was cheating because of something she had seen one night from her attic bedroom.

"I remember one night I woke up and I looked through the slats, as my cot was overlooking the living room. There was my mother stark naked in front of the fire, and I had never seen anything so mesmerizing in my life. There was a man sitting on the couch admiring her. It was not my dad. So when Bonnie told me about a decade ago that he had thrown her out — that she didn't leave us, she didn't abandon us — it wasn't until then that I put two and two together. My dad must have found out."

The friend who accompanied Donald on the Alaskan venture told Bonnie what had happened, and he also said that Donald and Diane passed each other on the street in Seattle about a year after she had left, but didn't say a word to each other.

"My dad used to say that it was always difficult for him whenever they'd go anywhere," said Saundra. "They'd enter a room and all eyes would land on her, and he felt that he had to be a man and defend his position a lot more than he wished he had to."

Diane's former Fairbanks consort Judy Morris said that "When (Diane) walked in a room, everybody quit eating or talking," and recalled an upsetting New Year's Eve party in Seattle, when Cecil's jealousy led to the police being called:

"We were in a hotel, just my husband and my son, and Cecil and Diane. There was somebody sat at our table, and he started flirting with Diane. Cecil took every glass on top of the table and started throwing them, and smashing them onto the dance floor. If somebody started flirting with her, he would just go into a rage."

In another interview, Saundra offered a more psychological insight into her mother:

"She was a charmer and that was her passion really, looking perfect, turning the heads of all these people and men and jealous women and all of that."

That pressure to be perfect affected Diane in a different way too.

"Her upbringing was such that… she had a tremendous inferiority complex. She didn't understand a lot of what was going on. My Grandmother Lee told me that when Diane and my dad would go to visit someone, she would sit in the car and look in the mirror and mess with her makeup until she thought it was perfect."

Saundra added that despite everything that happened, her father talked about Diane "until the day he died."

They weren't close, but back in the 1980s they had had an intense discussion about the marriage, and he said he felt he was "really green behind the ears, and there were a lot of things that he regrets. He didn't feel man enough to keep Diane in the first place, and I guess it's the old adage that if you know things aren't going to end well down the line or you're not capable of being a true partner in a relationship, a lot of times a person will take the initiative and break up with the other person first. That's what I think my dad did."

Donald remarried five more times, but apparently never forgot his first wife.

"He was with his last wife, and would still talk about Diane. She tolerated it because she loved him, and his rambling could go on and on towards the end, because he was a chronic alcoholic for years," said Saundra. Donald's "song" for Diane was "Take Five" by Dave Brubeck, and he apparently played it constantly, because for him, it was a musical expression of her.

"There were moments that are really happy, and then more intense, and there are other types of chords, and so on and so forth. She was everything. She had it all, and he just could not hold it. He knew he couldn't, he never got over it. He died at age 67 from liver failure and prostate cancer. Diane was an enigma. She was. My father talked about her until the day he died."

Diane and Donald's divorce was finalized on October 9, 1948 in Shelton, Washington, but despite the unhappy ending to their marriage, Diane kept a pocket Bible engraved DH Walker for years afterward. It emerged that she carried photographs of him and their daughters too.

After Diane and Cecil married they honeymooned in Honolulu, and their son was born in Fairbanks on Friday, August 18, 1950. They chose the name Marquam as a family tribute, though everyone called him Mark, but the joy over his birth was tempered just a few days later, when Diane learned that her grandmother Zoe had died aged 73.

Diane was Cecil's fifth wife, and she had only been married once before (or so everyone thought), but the truth was that Cecil was actually Diane's third husband.

Barely a month after her divorce from Donald, she and marine engineer William E. Aspee had been married in Seattle, though they were together for just 10 months. I couldn't find out much about him, though a 1956 article in New York's Sunday News suggested that their union failed because he "went to sea immediately" after they tied the knot.

The copies of the King County, Washington, ledger were badly faded and damaged, but I quickly found the details of their divorce. Cause Number 415382 was initially filed on December 21, 1949 — nearly three months after Diane and Cecil had been married.

Confused, I looked at my copy of Cecil and Diane's wedding license, and there it was in Cecil's own handwriting.

Her first name was listed as "Shelley", and it stated that she had been married just once before. That one marriage had ended in divorce in January 1947 — an incorrect date for both Donald and Aspee. Finally, the fact that her last name was listed as Walker, instead of Aspee, surely indicated she was trying to hide her past from Cecil, and maybe from the authorities.

Perhaps she had remembered how her mother had created a new persona, and used a temporary first name so she could get what she wanted — to marry Cecil.

On the full divorce documents Aspee was listed as the plaintiff, and Diane Walker Aspee (the correct use of her married names) the defendant. The 10-page document ended with the absolute decree dated April 18, 1950. It was noted that the defendant was not present on that final day, nor had she responded to the summons.

She couldn't, because she was in Fairbanks, and had been married to Cecil for over six months –and was pregnant with their child.

There were no children or property to divide between Diane and Aspee, but the cause was attributed:

"That the defendant has inflicted personal indignities upon the plaintiff to such an extent that it is no longer possible for plaintiff to live with defendant as husband and wife and that said personal indignities have rendered the life of the plaintiff burdensome and unbearable."

Whatever those "personal indignities" were, Diane had quickly moved on, and Saundra felt that she had given herself a different name so that Donald couldn't trace her –but then she mentioned another possibility.

"She led Cecil to believe that she wanted him to be the father of her children — that she didn't have any children — and that was part of the romance of their relationship. Later on, according to Mark (Marquam), or maybe through his fourth wife (Ethel) who was always digging, Cecil found out about Bonnie and I, and he confronted her."

However, in my 2021 interview with Judy, she said that Diane often talked about her two daughters, even though they weren't in contact, and that it wasn't a secret to Cecil.

Were Diane and Cecil even ever legally married? Even if it was just a rumor, it would surely have been addressed during the murder investigation, let alone during the subsequent legal tussles over Cecil's estate and custody of Marquam. The Aspee marriage wasn't a big secret, as it was mentioned in newspaper articles, though this legal snafu element of it didn't seem to appear in print until the *Sunday News* in 1956.

I found more new evidence relating to this: Saundra mentioned to me that Cecil and Diane were on their way back from a vacation in Australia when Diane was arrested at Seattle airport, and charged with bigamy and passing a bad check. Cecil's granddaughter Cathi McMurrin had a similar version: he was arrested in Seattle as he and Diane were about to board a ship for Alaska, because at the time he didn't even know Diane was married, let alone going through a divorce.

The *Compiled Laws of the Territory of Alaska* included bigamy under the same listing for polygamy, with the penalty for breaking it no more than seven years nor less than one year, but the *Sunday News* article claimed that Cecil made some phone calls, and made it go away.

I wondered about the reaction the Aspee divorce would have gotten if it had been revealed back in 1953, and I couldn't dismiss what Diane had done as an innocent mistake.

If Aspee was threatening her, why not tell Cecil about it? Maybe she felt that the marriage was so inconsequential it didn't need mentioning, especially since Cecil had gotten into trouble with love and law before. Besides, who checked marriage certificates? The likelihood of a paperwork fudge being discovered was negligible, and since she was starting a new life way up in Alaska, what was the real harm? It may have seemed romantic, and perhaps Cecil was so smitten that he didn't care, or Diane simply said that Shelley was her real first name, but she didn't use it.

Even so, I couldn't believe that Diane had abandoned her children, and I knew I had to meet them in person.

CHAPTER 14

Texas

Conroe, Texas is a city of about 85,000 residents some 40 miles north of Houston, and it was a pleasantly sunny day in October 2018 as I drove towards the large, tree-lined golf community where Saundra's eldest daughter London and her husband Dave lived. Saundra had a bad fall recently, breaking her right ankle in several places, and had to move in temporarily with them.

The house was large with many rooms and a swimming pool out back, though right now it was rather crammed with boxes and furniture due to Sandra's temporary stay. She had her own office here too, from which she was running an online vintage/wholesale clothes business.

Dressed in a rock band t-shirt and with long, white hair, London answered the door and led the way into the large kitchen, which was where I met their half dozen or so large but gentle Russian wolfhounds. We chatted for a while before Saundra came downstairs, and as soon as

she entered the room, I could immediately see the resemblance to her mother. With red lipstick, an animal skin-style sleeveless jacket and fashionable short, gray hair, she had inherited her mother's sense of style too.

She seemed a little reticent at first — about me, about why I had come all the way to Texas — but she had a number of family snaps on the table in the adjoining room, and I felt they were ready to discuss the past. Two of the photographs showed people in the traditional Scottish outfits of a kilt, feathered hats and sporrans, one of which was labeled William Walker 1869, and there was also a glamorous headshot of a young and long, dark, curly-haired Diane that I hadn't seen before.

There was also a coffee-stained *Seattle Post-Intelligencer* article from 1983 about the retirement of District Court Judge J. Edmund Quigley. The Wells case was mentioned in the interview, Quigley calling it "lurid" and saying that "all the men who had been intimate with (her) were going to be interviewed," and that "it was said that there were airplanes going 10 different directions, and only women and small children were left in town."

Quigley had been Diane's defense lawyer in Seattle, but now it sounded like he should have been leading the prosecution against her, and I was sad to see that even 30 years after her death she was still being named and shamed.

We sat down at the kitchen table and Saundra saw my laptop screensaver, which was a dramatic head shot of Diane.

"She drew people in with her magnetism. First her looks, then her magnetism — once anyone got within her field, you know?"

London told me she was actually christened Diane, but had changed her name because she "didn't like to think my grandmother was a murderer." She felt that it had been a stigma, even though the first time she heard about Diane, and about the murder, was when Saundra got a copy of Diane's death certificate.

"I just said out loud: 'I have another grandmother?'" said London.

It was Diane's daughter Bonnie who first found out how her mother had died.

"She found some records about it, and we confronted Grandma Lee," said Saundra, who added that she wasn't told about her grandmother Florence's death either.

"I could not believe that I had this precious relative I could ask a million questions of, and she had been just 50 miles away all that time. I planned for years and years and years to ask her a lot of things, and I only met her at her funeral."

Florence had a small container of Diane's possessions in her apartment, and Saundra said that she has always regretted not asking Grandma Lee for the $10 so it could be shipped to her, even though she knew the request would have caused an argument.

Over the next few hours we talked about all aspects of Diane's life, London suggesting that Cecil might have been a father figure for Diane, who had always needed validation and often got it through her looks, a trait she seemed to pass on to Saundra. London had once read Saundra's "baby book," a scrapbook for new parents (now lost), and a comment Diane wrote said she "wished Saundra had more eyebrows and eyelashes, because she was going to bring her to show the boys at the market."

There were also a number of moments when we surprised each other. Saundra seemed close to tears when I showed her Diane's will, which left everything to her, Bonnie, and Mark, and learning that Diane had spent time in an orphanage seemed to hit home too. "How frightening," she whispered.

Perhaps my most unsettling moments were when Saundra was talking about her childhood, and how it seemed that some of the unhappiness and trauma of that time had reverberated and passed down through the generations. She had five children with her first husband Don Comer — three girls and two boys — though their marriage was difficult and abusive.

One of the sons is currently in a low-security federal prison, while the other son, Gary, a musician and guitar maker, committed suicide at his studio in 2012. "His suicide note said music would be the death of him," said London, who explained that he hung himself with his guitar strap. "He struggled with life ever since I could remember, and just never seemed to make it in music," she added, saying that while he had been talking of suicide for some time, she still felt it came out of the blue.

London and Gary were very close, and his suicide note, final letters and favorite guitar inspired an album called *Beyond The Rain*, which London feels was a tribute to them surviving the cruelty of their father, who seemed to particularly dislike them because they were blonde like their mother (and like Diane, the big skeleton in the family closet). That artistic gene seems to run through the family, as London performs as a part of band WildeStarr, and, like her grandmother and great-grandmother, is also an artist.

Tragically, during the writing of this book another of Saundra's daughters died, seemingly of a heart attack, after a belated bipolar diagnosis and years of addiction to prescription drugs. Saundra talked honestly and openly about all of it, and about her third daughter, who was also struggling with addiction and schizophrenia.

What happened on the night when Cecil was murdered came up in conversation too, and London related her own experience of living alone and hearing the sounds of a break-in downstairs. "I owned a gun, but as I walked down the stairs, I just couldn't imagine firing it. I had been to shooting ranges, but I was terrified. I still couldn't imagine shooting someone."

It wasn't until the next day, for about an hour, that I really got to talk to Saundra alone. Among other things we talked more about her sister Bonnie, who had lived a rather unconventional and complicated life.

Also married five times, Bonnie had suffered the loss of a young child, suffered a nervous breakdown when her first husband came back from the conflict in Vietnam, and was estranged from another son. London was kinder, saying Bonnie was in fact a good mom, and that her younger "flower child" persona had simply clashed with Saundra's conservative, Mormon outlook.

Looking at snapshots of Saundra and Bonnie it's obvious they are sisters, and both look like their mother, but I was surprised when I read a Facebook post:

"Well, the DNA results are in...Bonnie & I are 99.82% full-blooded sisters!"

Saundra told me that she and her sister both disliked their father, and that at one time Bonnie "didn't want to believe we had the same father. She had doubted it our entire adult lives. In temperament, Bon and I have been 'off' with each other as long as I can remember, which was one of the reasons. Also, Bonnie had a suspicion that Donald's brother Bob might have had a fling with Diane, but DNA finally proved that wasn't the case."

Later, London told me that Bonnie designed jewelry and t-shirts for gift shops in Hawaii at one time, which shows that she shares the family's creative trait as well.

Diane's mother Florence never met her granddaughters, and Saundra felt that this was because Grandma Lee was "very possessive, plus she was our legal guardian. And maybe she didn't want me to know anything more about my mother." She also felt she was seen as free labor in the boarding houses that Grandma Lee ran. "I was like a Cinderella at her disposal," she recalled, adding how Grandma Lee always insisted that the two girls called her "mother."

"We were to introduce her as our mother. I hated that. It was a possession thing. She didn't want anybody to know that she was our grandmother."

Saundra's few happy times came when she went to church and talked to people her own age, and when she was with Uncle Dickie, her father's older brother, who was a teenager when she was around seven years old. They would play in the snow and pick crab apples, though she also recalled how Uncle Dickie, a little person, was bullied about his deafness and failing eyesight, and, shockingly, how he was accosted by one of the boarders.

She then confessed that she also had been accosted when she was eight years old by Grandma Lee's "favorite boarder." The guilty man was thrown out, leaving a traumatized Saundra to deal with her emotions, her boarding house duties, and responsibility for Bonnie and Uncle Dickie, whose physical condition was slowly deteriorating.

Soon after, they left Ogden for a brief stay in Flagstaff, Arizona, where Donald was selling Electrolux vacuum cleaners, and then moved on to San Jose in the South Bay area of San Francisco.

The location had changed, but Saundra and Bonnie were again living and working in a boarding house with Grandma Lee, and their father was rarely in touch.

"But there's been some suspicion that even if my dad wrote letters, Grandma Lee wouldn't have passed them on. Because I talked to my dad. Much later. And he said he did."

I told Saundra that Grandma Lee might have intercepted letters from Diane as well. Judy Morris remembered that Diane talked about her two daughters, so perhaps she had spent years trying to reach them after all? How many unanswered letters, birthday and Christmas cards did it take before Diane convinced herself that they didn't want to hear from her?

Even if this were true, Saundra later told me that she was angry with Diane, and remains so to this day, for leaving her.

After Uncle Dickie died following a series of heart attacks, Donald persuaded Grandma Lee into coming back to Phoenix, Arizona, where he was living with his second wife. The move was meant to be for a year, but "it didn't take my dad that long to accost me," said Saundra.

"He had hardly seen me in years, and years, and years. And here I am a 16-year-old. And he was going to give me driving lessons. Fine, great. And we went out in the desert outside of Phoenix and I was driving and he was reaching over: 'I want to know if you're like your mother.' That crap. So I was broken hearted. Because I hadn't seen him, I needed a parent, I wanted a parent, I wanted a father-daughter relationship. But that wasn't turning out. And then I saw him starting to make moves on Bonnie."

For a few moments, I couldn't speak. I didn't know what to say, and I felt both enraged and guilty for inadvertently digging all this up from the past.

Saundra graciously accepted my muttered apologies and told me that when she told Grandma Lee about what had happened, the pair of them, so often at odds with each other, came up with an escape plan.

"We enlisted the aid of a guy back in San Jose that was in love with me, one of Grandma Lee's boarders. He was like 21 and I was 16, and he was a journeyman lineman. I contacted him, he was really happy to hear from me. He agreed to do what we wanted to do, which was leave in the dark of night between Christmas and New Year. Just leave without telling my dad."

The lineman drove out to Phoenix, and they all left in secret.

"Then my dad called. And my Grandma Lee, I don't know what she said to him, but it wasn't enough."

She added that women definitely have a soft spot in their heart for their sons, as she had for Gary, but what happened next must have seemed like a huge betrayal: Grandma Lee took Saundra on the Greyhound bus back to Phoenix, and made her explain herself.

"And then my dad denied it!" said Saundra. "And now his second wife thinks I'm a pain in the association. And I was crying, and then we went back to San Jose. And I really resented Grandma Lee for putting me through that. And not having the balls, if you will, to just say she wants to protect me, to be on my side."

Saundra immediately started looking for a way out.

"I married young. I had to get out of that crazy boarding house thing. So my sister got my room, and more freedom. Grandma Lee had more freedom. And I was living in Berkeley and pregnant, and I was married Friday, June 13th, 1958. Friday the 13th."

Despite that notorious date, her marriage to Don was successful in the early days. They became heavily involved in custom homes and real estate, and while he worked at IBM in Los Gatos, she was down at the building department getting permits, making plans, and meeting with the architect.

"We had a bridge to build, we had roads and street lights to put in. We named the street after ourselves — Comer Drive in Saratoga — but then Don started getting really weird with me. He did. In every way."

Saundra told me about other abusive incidents that are unnecessary to detail here, but I did ask about her subsequent marriages. Saundra and Don divorced in 1969, and she married again for a few years each to Terry Topping and then William Knowles.

Somewhat echoing Diane's apparent dreams of Hollywood, at one time Saundra lived in Bavaria, then in West Germany, for several years. One day she and a friend were plucked from a rehearsal of *Jesus Christ Superstar*, put in period dress, and taken up on a plane to improvise playing American tourists flying over the Brandenburg Gate for a German television version of melodrama "Rich Man, Poor Man."

Until his death, Saundra was married to Earl Kinnaird, who she lived with in Las Vegas and still regularly posts happy memories and snapshots of. He was the only person that London says the children all happily called "dad".

CHAPTER 15

My Only Father

My Only Father
His Only Son

This was the inscription on Johnny's gravestone at the Houston National Cemetery. He had died in Spring, Texas in 1997, but who was this "only son"?

Back when he was a national story, Johnny's photograph was in *Life* and *Newsweek*. It also hit the pages of *Jet*, a magazine aimed at the African-American community, and saw him given the amusing moniker "the Don Juan of the northern Wastelands" in another. Indicted for murder alongside Diane, law enforcement kept investigating and scheduling his trial for years, yet he managed to almost disappear completely from the public eye after the case came to an end.

Born in Columbia in Marion County, Mississippi, on Monday December 15, 1919 to Eugene, a tailor, and Gladys, a teacher, Johnny had two older siblings; sister Ladell Willia, who was nearly three, and brother Roscoe Buford, who was nearly two. Not much is known of Johnny's early life, though it seems that his mother was a great influence on him.

In October 1941 he entered the US Army at Camp Shelby in Mississippi, and was released from duty a few days after his birthday in 1945 having reached the rank of Technician 5th Grade, which meant he would have been a Corporal on a higher pay grade. Sadly, his Official Military Personnel File was almost entirely destroyed in a fire in July 1973.

The last known address for Johnny was a large retirement community who weren't able to give out information about residents, but eventually Mike

Maddox at the Klein Texas Family History Center directed me to a Johnnie Condon Warren.

I had already found that differently-spelled name, and some dates matched up, but I had assumed it was a different person. If I had seen the 1951 Fairbanks phone book I would have known better, but at the time Maddox pointed out my obvious mistake; maybe Johnny had used or even formally changed his middle name from Condon to Charles?

Johnnie to Johnny was an understandable change of convenience too, and by comparing signatures on marriage certificates I was quickly able to uncover his marital and family history — and a mystery or two.

Like Cecil, Johnny was married five times in his life.

In early April 1943, 23-year-old Johnnie married 19-year-old Irma Leatha Reese in Maricopa, Arizona. Their relationship didn't last long, and less than a year later he married Viola James on March 9, 1944 in Lake County, Florida. That was a relatively short marriage too, as on February 4, 1948 he married Canadian-born Clara M. Malcolm in Seattle.

Clara stood by Johnny when he was arrested for murder, though that wasn't the first challenge they faced together. On July 15, just over five months after they had been married, they had a son who was born prematurely, and died within six hours.

Named only "Infant Warren" on the death certificate, the baby boy was cremated at the Fisher-Kalfus Funeral Home in Seattle, and their current incarnation as Dignity Memorial confirmed that he was interred in one of the crypt resting places. It had no name plate or metal vase on the front, and I was told it was a "community crypt" where multiple people would have been placed, especially stillborn or premature infants.

This unhappy event was new information about Johnny's past life, but not the story behind the gravestone inscription.

Perhaps this sad event prompted the move north to look for a fresh start, because by around 1949 they were living in Fairbanks and Johnny was working steadily in music. We know about this thanks to an article in the *FDNM* on July 28, 1951, which reported how Johnny, currently appearing at the Players Club, "is one of those guys that just can't leave the entertainment business. And the entertainment business is mighty glad of it."

More advertorial than interview, it reported that Johnny had been in the business for some 15 years and had been "one of Fairbanks' favorite vocalists" since he first arrived here some four years ago, perhaps then on tour.

According to the interview, he first began singing as a tot of four, and gained experience in a number of choral groups before making his debut at the tender age of 16 in New Orleans, fronting a 24-piece swing band, and becoming an instant success.

Before Fairbanks, his career had taken him to the West Coast and all over Seattle, where he met and joined a six-piece combo. The outfit swept Alaska by storm, but the group imploded, and all the other members went back to the States — except for Johnny. He liked Fairbanks from the day he arrived, the article said, and planned to stay indefinitely.

It was no wonder. Post-war Fairbanks had been enjoying a construction boom, and was overflowing with men who were working hard and wanted to play hard. There were many opportunities for a talented musician like him, and judging by the advertisements in the *FDNM*, Johnny could sing ballad-blues and "bounce" (a medium-tempo swing style), as well as play the drums, bass, piano and guitar. Sometimes he was a band leader, sometimes he helped supply the beats.

The article ended by saying that though Johnny has faced the inevitable ups and down and even "bid adieu" to the musical entertaining business, he keeps coming back.

"When I hear a live band, I get the urge to be up there with them," he said.

Johnny had worked behind-the-scenes too. He was involved with the fledgling Musician's Union in Fairbanks, and one of his duties would have included collecting union dues from his fellow performers.

Johnny's time in Fairbanks saw his family growing too.

When he was arrested in Oakland, Clara was reported as being pregnant, but there was no archival reference to the birth of another child. Statistically women who suffer a stillborn child are more likely to have it occur again, especially if the previous pregnancy was between 20-30 weeks (which could have been possible, even if Clara was newly-pregnant when they were married).

I already knew that Johnny and Clara had adopted a daughter — Susanna, who accompanied him on his drive to Oakland — but I didn't know the very unusual circumstances in which it happened. That story began in a jail cell after Johnny had been brought back to Fairbanks from Oakland in late November 1953. He had ended up sharing the space with an inmate named Donald Pratt, who was accused of killing his girlfriend, 26-year-old Annette Mae Wood, at the Talk of the Town earlier that year.

The *FDNM* headline reported that cab driver Pratt opened fire with a .45 caliber pistol at Annette, who was the hat check girl and also a clerk at the Piggly Wiggly store, then chased her down as she ran bleeding into the busy club. She was hit in the arm, chest and abdomen, and died in the hospital the next afternoon. An off-duty police officer was also hit in the leg by one of the bullets that passed through Wood, though he survived.

After Pratt was overpowered by a number of shocked and outraged bar patrons, he apparently said:

"Did I get her?"

When he was arrested, he muttered that Annette had been keeping company with another man, and that the only thing he regretted was "accidentally hitting that cop."

For a moment I wondered if that "man" was Johnny, who also worked at the Piggly Wiggly and gigged at the Talk of the Town, but a document found among Wood's probate paperwork gave a different answer.

Scribbled in pencil on a blank postcard and dated March 25, 1953 were Annette's instructions that, in the event of her death, Susanna was to be adopted by Johnny and Clara Warren. This suggested that she had already suffered at the hands of a jealous Pratt, and was preparing her two friends for the worst. No wonder the *Seattle Times* reported that Johnny and Pratt ending up as temporary cellmates was causing officials some concern.

Johnny and Clara officially adopted 5 year old Susanna Denise on September 17, and the process would have been coming to a conclusion around the time that Johnny and Diane allegedly first met at the Fairbanks Country Club.

With Diane and her mother both having experience of adoption and the orphanage system, it's easy to imagine this was something she and Johnny might have discussed — maybe even connected emotionally about. Perhaps Diane also hinted that she understood about Annette's unhappy domestic life.

After almost two years in a psychiatric institution, Pratt was convicted of second-degree murder and sentenced to 15 years in prison, though sadly I was never able to find out what happened to Susanna. However, I did learn that Johnny had a biological child — a son named John Charles Warren, who was born February 20, 1981.

John called me back within a few hours, and one of the first things he asked me was the middle name of the man I was looking for. It was Condon I said, and he replied that yes, he was Johnny's youngest and only living child. He spoke briefly about his parents, noting that they had a rather volatile marriage which did not end well, and that "he was a better father than a husband."

John lived in Sugar Land, about 20 miles south west of Houston, and we arranged to meet at a coffee shop in the Sugar Land Town Square Mall. I realized I didn't have any idea what he looked like, but once I approached him and he smiled, I recognized his father's face.

He was about the same age as Johnny was in the 1953/1954 photographs, and told me that he had been born when Johnny was 61:

"He didn't show his age as much as people would think, because even as I was growing up as a kid, you could definitely tell he was older, but when I was playing baseball, meeting my friends at social events, he would still kind of look like a gentleman in his 50s."

John said that his father may have had some Native American roots, and that his skin color was known as "Redbone," a lighter black with some brownish-reddish freckles. "Redbone" is a term used in much of the southern United States to denote a multiracial individual or culture, and Johnny was born in Mississippi.

We noted that Diane and three of Johnny's four wives had been white, and John explained that his mother Ellen met Johnny at Rudi Lechner's, a restaurant that's still in North Houston, where she was a waitress and he was a regular customer. John said that he and his father had had a good relationship, though it did face some obstacles after his parents divorced when he was around eight years old.

"And so after that, there was separate custody, separate housing, separate living situations. My mother had custody, so I would do the every Wednesday, every other weekend type of thing, rotating holidays. But his treatment of me was always very fair."

He felt that his father was very loving toward him, and that Johnny carried on working into his later years with a shipping/logistics company. He added that he only knew what his mother had told him, and what he had read after his death.

"My father and I didn't really speak a whole lot about his childhood. Whether that was his choice or just coincidence, I don't know."

It was new information to John that his father had been married several times before, and he joked about his own two divorces:

"So I'm following suit, is what you're saying."

He did however meet Johnny's siblings; sister Willia, and brother Roscoe and his wife. He recalled the family spending one Christmas in Seattle with Roscoe and his family, and said the brothers seemed to get on well.

A strong connection between father and son was music.

"He did love music. I mean, he was a big influence of why I love it so much in that he would expose me to a lot of jazz music… big band and blues and things."

John didn't remember seeing instruments in the house, but had "a few vague memories of him going to some jam sessions when I was maybe between nine and twelve years old perhaps. Thankfully for me, one thing I can carry on is, I did inherit his singing ability."

John had singing lessons when he was young, was in choir through high school, and latterly auditioned for "American Idol" and "The Voice." He said he enjoyed singing, even if he felt he wasn't very accomplished or accredited, and regretted not developing it into more of a career path.

Sadly, Johnny never really knew much about his son's musical abilities:

"Unfortunately not. Because he passed away when I was 15 almost 16, so

I was really starting to become more confident and outgoing with my singing…I'm more of a "shower superstar" and (performed) to a couple of friends here and there."

But his father did see him perform in a couple of choir concerts in his freshman or sophomore years, which John said was really affirming, adding that both his parents supported his music and sports endeavors, Johnny even coaching one of his baseball teams.

"He did whatever he could in my respect to make me feel loved and wanted. I mean, I always had presents under the tree. I always had food in the house and lunch at schools, and he did his best to be part of my life as much as possible."

It was around this time that we first discussed what he had referred to as "the event."

John knew nothing about his father's involvement in Cecil's murder until he read the November 1953 edition of *Life* that was found among Johnny's possessions after his death.

"I was so taken aback that my mother had never mentioned it. And I had gone to her basically kind of with this magazine in hand saying 'What gives? When did you know about this?' And her recounting what little she knew about the case, and that she's never really looked into it and researched it. Maybe she just didn't want to know."

She said that Johnny had never mentioned it to her, yet he had kept that copy of *Life* for nearly 45 years.

"I thought many things," said John. "My mind was racing about, okay, who is this woman? What was their involvement? What could my dad have been a part of? Was he actually the gunman? Did he commit the murder? You hear: my father, affair, murder. So naturally, you try to not think negatively about it, but your mind just starts wondering, because you have so little to go on."

Inadvertently raising one of the issues that might have been a factor in the Wells' marriage (and maybe the murder), he continued:

"And my parents, from what I remember being aware of, had their challenges. Husbands and wives have arguments. They had physical arguments sometimes, but I never necessarily associated my father to be a very violent person and able to commit a murder. Now, was he maybe the type of person in self-defense to do something? I don't know. Naturally most people might be, but even in his everyday life, he was never that type of personality to be overly excitable or want to incite arguments or be that physical with people."

I explained briefly about Johnny and Diane's relationship, and how Johnny had left Fairbanks on the day of the murder.

"It looked incriminating," admitted John, adding that his father kept guns in the house when he was growing up.

"My mother hated them. When they were divorced and he had his own place, there was a shotgun there. There was a handgun (too). And he didn't really expose me much to handguns... he was very private about them, kept them locked and away and such. I didn't really get to handle them until he passed. My mother very quickly ushered me to a gun show to sell them."

But he admitted that he had kept one of his father's weapons, a short-barrel shotgun that was perhaps a Winchester.

CHAPTER 16

"Plain and simple case
of murder"

Fairbanks, Alaska — Tuesday November 3, 1953

The same November day that the arrest warrants were issued for Diane and Johnny, Chief of Police Danforth received the two boxes of evidence back from the FBI. It was accompanied by laboratory report PC-36978 GX, which had been signed at the top by J. Edgar Hoover himself; a summary had been sent a week before, and it noted that the mattress blood sample and the woolen cap had not been received.

That was a break in the chain of evidence, but the notes on the report about Q1, the .380 bullet taken from Cecil's pillow, seemed very promising. Specifically, the rifling characteristics on it indicated that it was fired from a worn barrel, that there were good individual marks (e.g., grooves or lands) for identification matching the inside of that barrel, and the firing pin impression suggested that a .380 Italian Beretta semi-automatic pistol was "most likely" the weapon used.

The cartridge and bullet were identified as being manufactured by Western, and a small drawing in the report's draft notes indicated the marks from the breech and ejector that could be used to identify the suspect weapon — if it was found.

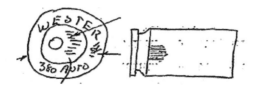

As for the latent fingerprints (as opposed to patent ones, which are left behind in blood, paint or other non-human substances), the notes say that only the whisky bottle was tested; there were none on the drinking glass, and the ones on the vodka bottle had no value. Fingerprint cards from Cecil, Diane and Johnny had been sent for comparison, and while four of the fingerprints on the whisky bottle were Diane's, two were still unidentified, but weren't a match for Cecil or Johnny. A later test with Herbert Mensing, the Wells' dinner guest the evening before the murder, came back negative too.

As for the blood testing, the results weren't encouraging here either. Cecil's blood (group 0) had been found on the pillowcase and Diane's (group A) on the carpet and on her left shoe, but there was insufficient to produce a result on blood on the wall, Diane's right shoe, and the pressure cooker button. There was nothing significant on the threads and flowerpot pieces either.

From the very beginning, Diane's involvement in the affair and the murder had been hotly debated. After her arrest she vowed to find the killer and dismissed Johnny's words as "complete lies," saying that only ever him for two "luncheon meetings," and that was because he had threatened to expose something from her or Cecil's past.

But what secret might he have known?

Johnny was still under arrest in San Francisco and fighting extradition, but an encouraged Danforth wrote back to the FBI sending them 24 .380 caliber cartridges (named as K1A, K1B etc.) to be compared with Q1 and Q2. The FBI file doesn't explain how, but the cartridges were obtained from Robert Still, the former owner of the .380 Italian Beretta (serial number 648506, or what I called possible Gun #1).

This gun was believed to have become the property of Johnny Warren, wrote Danforth, and if any of the 24 could be linked to the markings found on Q1 or Q2, it would "strengthen our efforts in proving that it was the death weapon."

But then, oddly, Danforth writes that the Beretta had not been found "and we have not located records which show the chain of ownership to Warren."

It's a stark contrast from one sentence to the next, but it seems to show that Danforth and DA Stevens believed Johnny could have been the shooter, or at least supplied the weapon that killed Cecil. Danforth asked for these new results to be air mailed to him (an expensive request), and said that Q1 and Q2 are on their way back to the FBI laboratory. He asked that they keep them there for future reference or until called for in connection with court trial.

The story was still making headlines across the world, and on November 11 it ran in muck-raking British tabloid the *Daily Herald* under the headline "Murder trial wife on bail". Closer to home, *Newsweek* of November 16 titled their short piece "Drummer and Blonde."

On November 18 the *Seattle Times* reported that lawyer J. Edmund Quigley was joining Diane's defense team, and he was quoted as saying that "I cannot find one shred of evidence capable of bringing Mrs. Wells to trial," and added that "the police work in this case is nothing to be proud of… this sort of thing makes people lose faith in police operations."

On November 20, as temperatures dipped below zero, Danforth was blindsided by another attack. Having finished their annual duties the grand jury in Fairbanks had made a number of recommendations — including that he should resign or be fired, as in their estimation he was unqualified for the job as Chief of Police. No explanation was given by the jury foreman, and a clearly-shocked Danforth told the *FDNM*:

"For what reason?"

Another recommendation had been that Ted Stevens should be permanently appointed. He was effusively praised as honest, capable, exacting… willing, conscientious and above all honest" (note the two mentions of honesty).

It must have been an utter humiliation for Danforth.

There was one last rebuke too, when they formally recommended that the Crime Squad should be reassembled, ideally with a member of the military if possible, and reorganized to deal with all violent felonies (burglary, arson, grand larceny, murder, manslaughter and others). The squad should be independent, with their reports going straight to the DA, and hopefully this would prevent any other people from accessing crime scenes.

Barely in the job a month, newly-appointed US Marshal Al Dorsh Jr was reported to have every intention of carrying out these suggestions, and a series of advertisements about car vandalism in the *FDNM* in late 1954 showed the Crime Squad was operating again, at least on some level. Mayor Rivers was throwing his support behind the idea too, and an editorial suggested that "Chief of Police Danforth (or his successor) extends full cooperation" to the city.

Danforth couldn't have missed the inclusion of the words "or his successor".

Both Diane and Johnny entered pleas of not guilty, and on November 25 the federal building was full of curious members of the public as Judge Harry E. Pratt refused the request from her lawyers, Walter Sczudlo and Charles Clasby, to change the venue of the trial.

They knew that the optics of Diane and Johnny being anywhere near each other was always going to be the focus of everyone, including the jury. Every gesture, whether it was a smile, a whisper or a sigh, would be analyzed and interpreted, plus there was always the possibility that friends and relatives of Cecil, Diane and Johnny would have to share space in the public gallery.

Sczudlo and Clasby also felt that racial prejudice could hurt their client, and that the media were more focused on her so-called social misconduct than who actually shot Cecil. Sczudlo noted dryly that there were "more people in the courtroom listening to the hearing than there were at Cecil Wells' funeral," and spoke of the lurid stories that had appeared in the States and across the territory.

Stevens argued back that this area was known for having very little racial prejudice, and so any such thoughts had been raised as a "natural incident" to a crime of this nature. In many ways this was true, as the local African-American population was very small, with the large Native Alaskan community instead facing decades of discrimination. He added that people weren't "lynched in Fairbanks as they do in the south," and that there has been no proof "the community hates Diane Wells, or that she has been hated for years."

It was a dubious example, but Johnny's lawyers had requested a separate trial too. It seemed like he was trying to distance himself from Diane and the murder, while she was more concerned that she wasn't going to get a fair trial in her home town.

On that same day, Diane's lawyers made another specific request. Since there was no legal distinction in the United States between being a principal or an accessory in a first- or second-degree murder charge, could she either be formally charged with the murder, charged with being an accomplice, or she and Johnny charged as co-conspirators? They couldn't both have fired the fatal bullet, so a distinction should be made, the lawyers argued.

They wanted to avoid the possibility of Diane and Johnny testifying against each other, though Stevens felt that determining who actually pulled the trigger was secondary. More than that, the Territory of Alaska did not have a conspiracy statute, and so since Johnny and Diane were indicted together, they "must stand and answer for the crime together," insisted Stevens.

He then stated that the case was circumstantial, but "We have here just a plain and simple case of murder, of two people who committed murder and which the Government will prove, that they committed murder."

Johnny and Diane were both out on $5,000 bail (murder being a bailable offense in Territorial Alaska), but they were soon set to meet again — in the courtroom.

Cecil and Diane seemed to have a whirlwind romance. A pioneering Alaskan businessman, he was 20 years older than she, with several marriages already behind him. After meeting in Seattle, they moved to Fairbanks in 1949, with son Marquam coming along the next year. They traveled extensively too, visiting countries including Mexico, Brazil and Peru.

Cecil, Diane and Marquam moved into two top floor apartments in the Northward Building, the $2.5m luxury "skyscraper" in downtown Fairbanks. One of their neighbors, William Colombany, ran a dance studio, and they signed up for lessons.

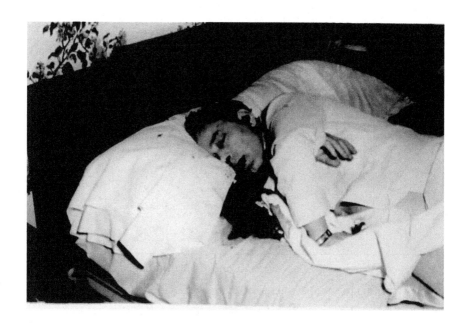

Crime scene photos showed that Cecil Wells had been killed while he slept, and police initially announced he had been bludgeoned to death. A bruised Diane told investigators that two men had broken into their eighth floor apartment, gaining access via the door connecting 814 and 815 and causing the picture frame (above) to fall. Police determined the murder weapon was likely to be an Italian Beretta .380 – but now they had to find it.

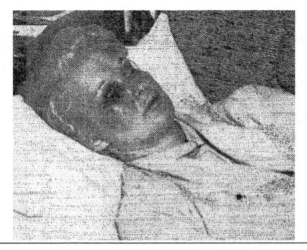

Her eyes blackened and her face cut and swollen, Diane lies on the sofa after returning to the apartment she shared with Cecil and Marquam. She later spoke to *Life* magazine about her experience, but only returned to the family home one more time after the murder. To many, her injuries suggested something other than a burglary that had turned violent.

Chief of Police E.V. Danforth was skeptical about Diane's account from the start, as was the new Fairbanks District Attorney, Ted Stevens. With Alaskan statehood always on the political agenda, finding the killer was essential, and could make or break a career – but the men soon clashed, and the investigation made several crucial mistakes.

THE
Barbary Coast
EXOTIC
WANDA
With her sizzl-
ing tempting in-
terpretations of
terpsichores.
LOVELY
CANDY
Even when you
see it, you won't
believe it.

– SHOWTIME –
12 Midnight
2:30 am, 5:00 am
Music for listening and
dancing by Johnny and
the Combo.

Parties Are Our Specialty

Large or Small

WE HANDLE EVERYTHING...
Orchestra Available for Larger Banquets

DANCE TO JOHNNY WARREN'S
BAND EACH SATURDAY NIGHT!

The Country Club
DIAL 3270 For Reservations

Burlesque shows were a regular feature at clubs and bars in Fairbanks. Johnny Warren played at many of them, and it was during one night at the Fairbanks Country Club, when he yawned as the performer began her striptease, that Diane Wells first noticed him. A photograph of that night (below, with helpful arrows) was seen in newspapers and magazines around the world.

Johnny Warren was accused of murder alongside Diane Wells, and when he told police that they were lovers, it became a bigger scandal. However, US Marshal Frank Wirth (left) said publicly that he thought Johnny was innocent, and his unpublished memoir revealed more of his suspicions about the crime.

Later in life Johnny had a son (right), and though they shared a love of music, he never talked about the years he lived under suspicion of Cecil's murder. John only learned about it when he read an old copy of *Life* magazine he found in his father's possessions.

 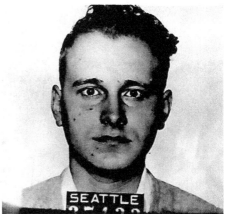

The photograph of Diane sitting on the lap of William Colombany added fuel to the suspicion that their relationship was more than just close friends. Colombany's life was largely a mystery, but new evidence revealed he abandoned his children, and had an even darker past than his short period of jail time in connection to the Cecil Wells murder.

Pulp magazines like *Front Page Detective* and *Official Detective* lavished coverage on the Cecil Wells murder story, especially the fact that it involved money, sex, race, and what one of them christened "the most beautiful woman in Alaska."

As well as being covered in the pages of *Newsweek*, *Life* and *Jet*, the story also went as far afield as England and Australia. Diane fled to Los Angeles with young Marquam to try and escape the cameras – and the gossip.

Diane wanted to spare Marquam the publicity of a scandalous trial. It led to a short custody battle for the "millionaire" four year old boy, who was cruelly dubbed the "Murder Orphan".

Bottom left: the Drake Hotel today, and on the right the Hollywood Plaza Hotel in the 1930s.

Left: sisters Saundra and Bonnie Walker with Grandma Lee. On the right, Saundra today in Conroe, Texas. Below, with Saundra and her daughter – Diane's granddaughter – London.

CHAPTER 17

The Unpublished Memoir

Despite Danforth's brazen disregard for Diane's story about a home invasion, many people believed her "not guilty plea" — or at least that she wasn't the only person involved. One of them was Deputy U.S. Marshal Frank Wirth, who accompanied the handcuffed Johnny back to Fairbanks in the early morning chill of November 24, and hinted to reporters that there was a man from Alaska of "substantial status" who was connected to the case.

Wirth said that he felt Johnny hadn't pulled the trigger, and was "withholding information because of fear of his own safety or because he is covering up for someone else." The *San Francisco Chronicle* added that Wirth said he had the information which, when fitted in with evidence, would be enough to sew up the case, though "Warren may still be an accessory to the murder."

These suspicions were widely reported, and while Johnny himself made no comment, Wirth told reporters that he expected the arrest of the new, third suspect ("a white man in Alaska"), within the next few days. Chances were then very good that the charges would be reduced against his currently-handcuffed passenger.

Third Suspect Faces Arrest In Alaska Slaying

Well over six feet and rather tough-looking, Wirth added an ominous threat that he surely hoped this new suspect might read:

"I know who he is and he knows I know."

Cecelia Wirth (née Richard), is one of Wirth's six children. She lives in Kenai, Alaska, and recalled hanging out with her friends in the Northward Building as a child. She told me her father had kept records of some of his cases — including his unpublished memoir — and kindly sent me them in early 2018.

Completely new evidence relating to the murder, the package also included some original photographs, a telephone call transcript, pages of the *Sunday News* article, a Seattle PD mugshot marked as "a suspect in the Wells case," and the three typewritten pages of his memoir. Though they were written many years later, Wirth had been heavily involved in the Wells case, so his private thoughts about it carried a great deal of weight.

Wirth writes about receiving the tip from Tommy Wright's son that Diane was "fond" of Johnny, and his subsequent assignment to collect Johnny in San Francisco. He also states that his expenses, perhaps other out-of-pocket ones, were paid by Jim Messer, Cecil's business partner and the purchaser of his Garden Island home:

"He really wanted to find Cecil's murderer," said Cecilia.

Messer's determination to find his friend's killer was confirmed by his daughter Patty Wagner Messer, who works in operations for the Alaska State Troopers, and said that her father "reminisced many times about his boss and friend... they (had) spent many evenings in each other's homes." She said that much later, perhaps in the 1980s, Messer even hired a private detective to look into the case and had assembled a collection of notes, papers and micro cassettes — seemingly including his conversations with Wells family members — and was planning to use them as the basis for a book.

Unfortunately, the notes and micro cassettes had gone partly missing over the years, and then were lost completely when her older sister unwittingly hired a fake removal company; police found the empty and ransacked van in the desert.

Patty said that her father met Diane a number of times, but didn't like her. "He was firm in his belief that Diane did it," she said, adding that "Cecil basically took him in, and Jim would have done anything for him. Once he even got up at 4am to fix his furnace. I think really he wanted closure."

The affection seemed to be mutual, as Cecil's will directed that Messer was to be given the first chance to buy Wells Alaska Motors, and Messer and a business partner did so. They changed the name to Aurora Motors, announcing it with a large ad that featured a jolly baby "and a new name for an old firm."

Alaska collector, historian and philanthropist Candy Waugaman recalled having coffee with Jim Messer and other friends, and said that he talked about the murder "every day." She also mentioned that right after the murder, Messer employed Johnny to wash cars at the car dealership. An act of kindness that was never mentioned in the newspapers, it wasn't the only public declaration of support that the alleged co-conspirator received in his community after his indictment.

The memoir opens by stating that "Cecil Wells was killed by an Italian Beretta handgun."

In the following paragraphs Wirth lays out the bare facts of the case, and notes how "Diana" was taken to the hospital and that Sally Martin didn't ride in the ambulance, but instead walked over the Cushman Street Bridge to St. Joseph's Hospital. He further mentions how he searched the Northward Building, and how he later "took in and checked many Berettas for ballistics, including sending them to the FBI lab."

He then makes a startling suggestion — and implication:

"I began to wonder if the Beretta had found its way into the Chena Slough."

Wirth noted that the Chena Slough had been used as a dumping ground since at least spring 1944, when he and other members of the Justice Department took slot machines confiscated from illegal gambling raids and threw them into the water. Gambling was a long-term problem in the city, and one long-time Fairbanks resident remembered how she and her husband rented a house and found several slot machines in the basement.

Pronounced "sloo", a slough is a river side-channel. There is a 13-mile-long stream called the Chena Slough several miles east of downtown, and it would have been ideal for dumping slot machines (or anything else for that matter). Wirth however wrote in his memoir that he meant what was now known as the Chena River, with the Cushman Street Bridge crossing it.

Wirth gives a brief history of the boxy, steel bridge, which had just opened for traffic a couple of months before the murder; Cecil and Diane would probably have been at the event. He adds that this bridge was later relocated to the coastal town of Nome, some 500 miles west, and reassembled over the Kuzitrin River in 1958. It's still called the Cushman Street Bridge today.

No waters in Fairbanks were searched for the murder weapon, but Mitch Osbourne, a certified master diver and fishery biologist with the US Fish & Wildlife Service, said that if it had been thrown off the bridge, the gun could still be in the water, even today.

He has traveled all over Alaska at the request of various law enforcement agencies to find everything from missing persons to vehicles, guns, knives, wallets and wedding rings — and once parts of an old paddlewheel steamer — and he has dived around this bridge a number of times.

The water there is "dark water" (meaning little or no visibility), and that it could flow pretty fast at 1 1/2 to 3 knots, or faster around the pilings. The water is normally only 4-8 feet deep, and surprisingly, he said that 90% of the time a missing or disposed-of item is often close to where law enforcement estimate it might be — usually in a cleared search area of around 25-50 feet.

Aside from the memoir, the most memorable item that Cecelia sent was a photograph taken at San Francisco Airport, just before Johnny was brought back to Fairbanks. He's handcuffed, his hands out in front of him and not covered with his coat like in other photographs, while next to him, with a half-finished cigar in his right hand, is Frank Wirth.

And they're both smiling — even laughing — together.

On arrival back in Fairbanks, the *FDNM* reported that Wirth had said Johnny was an "enjoyable traveling companion… not moody or sullen in any way." Cecelia said that her father was a keen guitarist and singer, and a shared love of music might have bonded the pair, because in that photograph they look for all the world like two friends sharing a joke, rather than a suspect being extradited to face murder charges.

Wirth died aged 86 in 2007, and while this never-published photograph of him and Warren together may not represent anything significant, the fact that he kept it (and the statements he made about his belief in Johnny's innocence or near-innocence), do seem to say more than pages of testimony might have done. Wirth was even reported as saying:

"I liked Johnny Warren. He didn't kill anybody!"

There were also more compelling suspects than Johnny.

An unidentified witness had given a statement to Wirth that "tied a Fairbanks businessman in suspiciously with the case… The man had the Colombany Dance Studio in Fairbanks and was known to be very close to Mrs. Wells."

Looking almost like Marilyn Monroe in the picture, Diane is sitting on the lap of a man with curly black hair. He's grinning devilishly as he looks at the camera, his chin resting on her right shoulder, and they're clearly very close. When I first saw it, I thought it was Cecil and Diane, but then I looked at the caption: it was her and William Colombany.

His name came up frequently in the investigation, but it seemed that very little was known about him besides his South American ancestry and his dancing career. Then, in a series of phone calls with Colombany's granddaughter Norma Lucy Fullon (née Colombany) who lived in Riverbank, California, I learned some new evidence about his family history:

"My mom is still secretive about him, and really doesn't like talking about it," she said, "But I barely knew his name."

William (or Guillermo) Barillas Colombany was the second child of Rebecca Linares and Moises Barillas, who married in El Salvador in 1918. They also had a daughter, Marina, who was born in Jutiapa, Guatemala on November 11, 1920, while William was born in Jutiapa on Monday February 5, 1923.

The family was a mix of Italian and El Salvadorean backgrounds, which might explain why Guillermo's last name wasn't Barillas, but came from his grandfather Carlos Colombani, as was Italian custom, and saw Barillas moved up to be his middle name. Though it was changed or maybe Anglicized, its roots were in the Latin "colombe," which means "dove," and it has its roots in Genoa, Italy, when the dove was seen as a symbol of the Holy Spirit.

Interestingly, Rebecca's death certificate lists her father as being from France, and the French cities of Savoy and Nice, some 100 miles from Genoa, were annexed by Italy in 1860. Maybe the family was historically caught up in that, or maybe, much more simply, he simply changed the order of the names himself.

Norma explained to me that, as far as she knew, Colombany left the family home in El Salvador in the late 1940s or early 1950s, leaving behind his wife Josefina, a nurse, and daughters Sonia, born in 1942, and Norma Lydia, who was born in 1945.

This tallied somewhat with official records. He had registered for the WWII draft in San Francisco in October 1945, just after major hostilities had ended, though like Johnny, his full military record had been destroyed in the 1973 fire. His US Naturalization Record dated December 18, 1946, when he was admitted to the US via Ancón in Panama, had the same San Francisco address. His sister Marina was living in San Francisco then, too.

But then Norma told me the reason for his sudden departure from El Salvador:

"Okay, this is what I found out through one of my aunts, okay? My grandfather left my grandmother for another woman, and that girlfriend then killed my grandmother."

Had Colombany been connected to another murder, just a few years before Cecil was killed? If this allegation were true and had come to light at the time, it would have put him firmly, and perhaps damningly, in the spotlight as the "third suspect."

Unfortunately Norma had no idea what the girlfriend/alleged murderer's name was, but she was certain:

"She killed my grandmother Josefina."

This secret had been buried very deep, and Norma had originally been told something very different:

"Before I talked to you, I was under the impression that my grandmother Josefina had passed away of pneumonia. Because that's what my mom said... and I don't even think my mom knew, because she was also told that she died of an illness."

There are several possible reasons for this deception, but it really affected Norma's life because in the wake of the murder, Josefina's eldest sister Maria adopted the abandoned daughters Sonia and Norma Lydia, and became "grandma" to them. They shared many tearful phone calls after Norma and her parents moved to the States, but never actually saw each other in person again, something that Norma still regrets:

"In my country, when somebody is murdered or something, one of your children pays for it," she said, suggesting that this was almost a curse on her family.

Colombany didn't even attend Josefina's funeral, said Norma, and there were no arrests in relation to the crime. Privately, she refers to him as "Charles Manson":

"You know how Manson plotted to kill these people, but he never did it — he had his accomplice people do it? That's what my grandfather did. Like a mastermind."

Locating accurate El Salvadorean police records from the 1950s was impossible, especially without dates and names, but I asked Norma if she knew how her grandmother Josefina was killed. At different times she said both strangling and stabbing, but despite the sad stories she was able to make a joke:

"You know how people have skeletons in their closet? Well Hell's Bells, James, I have a whole bunch. You want some? I have plenty!"

Whether he was on the run or not, Colombany ended up 5,800 miles away from El Salvador.

In the early 1950s he and Florence Rae Bailey opened a dance school in Anchorage, Alaska, and on a rather cool March 7, 1952, they were married in Reno, Nevada. Colombany hired several people to help them teach, but Bailey took over day-to-day matters when he became the owner/manager of the Ambassador Club.

Their shared love of dancing wasn't enough however, and the marriage only lasted just over a year.

Their divorce case was number A-8919, and was heard in Anchorage. The complaint read in part "That there is an incompatibility of temperament between the plaintiff and the defendants; that the likes, dislikes and temperaments of the parties of this action are not alike and are greatly divergent; that there is no common ground between the parties, and that it has become impossible for the plaintiff and the defendant to live together as husband and wife."

In short, Colombany and Bailey did not get on — at all.

He didn't appear at any of the hearings since he had already arrived in Fairbanks, and was ordered to pay the $350 attorney's fees. He quickly sold the Anchorage dance school to his now ex-wife, and in April 1953 proclaimed his new Fairbanks dance school open for business.

He hired two assistants, and began offering lessons in the waltz, foxtrot, samba, swing, rumba and tango. With so many clubs in town and such an upscale location, Cecil and Diane were probably just two of his many clients.

The advertisement noted that Colombany was from Guatemala, and that he had served as a public relations officer and military attaché to the American Embassy during WWII. The US State Department had no record of him, but he might have been an outside contractor, so it's hard to know if this claim was true or not. It might explain the 1946 trip via the Panama Canal, but either way it would have had some cachet in a military town like Fairbanks. It also sounded like he might be a useful person to know if you got caught in a jam.

Nevertheless, William Colombany was the only person to go to trial in relation to the murder of Cecil Wells. But that happened much later, and came about in the strangest way.

CHAPTER 18

Bloody Pajamas

Fairbanks, Alaska - November 30-December 9, 1953
Los Angeles, California - December 10, 1953-February 12, 1954

THE CASE OF THE BEAT-UP BLONDE

That was the headline about a photo-play recreation in the November 30 weekly edition of *Life* magazine.

At that time it was in its heyday, with a print run of several million and a reach of several million more readers. That the murder was featured in their pages meant it was a big story, and they didn't pull any punches in their coverage.

The article began with the images of Diane lying on the sofa, only this time the photographs were closer-up and showed more of the damage to her face.

With those two black eyes it's hard not to look at the photographs and wince, and after she left hospital people probably looked at her with a mixture of sympathy — and suspicion. It hardly seemed possible that a small flowerpot, empty or full of earth (even two of them), could do such damage. A broken nose could produce black eyes perhaps, but she said she had been hit on the head.

Those unsettling photographs were in stark contrast to when *Life* had actually visited Fairbanks. Fully recovered, hair done and dressed in a fashionable black suit, she recreated for their photographer how she had been attacked by one of the "thugs" while the other was killing Cecil.

118

An uneasy-looking Jack Ryan stood in as her assailant, grabbing her from behind and putting a hand over her mouth, and then reaching for the unusual nearby weapon. Another more melodramatic photograph showed Diane peeking out from behind the safety chain (of apartment 719, not the Wells'), the text alongside saying that she was "free but fearful" of a return visit by the men she said had killed her husband and attacked her. The article ended with a question that had already occurred to many people, not just *Life* magazine:

"Who if not thugs beat up Diane Wells so viciously?"

POLICE CHIEF DANFORTH RESIGNS

The very same day that *Life* hit the newsstands, E. V. Danforth resigned as the Chief of Police.

His resignation letter stated that his efforts to get the police department organized had impaired his health, but the decision was in the interest of local harmony noted the *Seattle Times*, who added that he had been coming under fire for his handling of the case, most recently from the Fairbanks grand jury.

Jet reported that Danforth scoffed at the "hot air" talk of a third suspect, and in an *Anchorage Times* interview the "handsome one-time San Diego policeman" said there were secret avenues of inquiry in the investigation. For a man who had once been addressed by J. Edgar Hoover as "My Dear Chief" he was understandably bitter, adding that Fairbanks officials "chickened out in the end," and that he was a victim of circumstance and petty jealousy. He was also critical of the current "haphazard" investigation that he was sure he would have "wrapped up."

Or perhaps not.

He had sent the 24 cartridges to the FBI some two weeks earlier, and promised to mail the Q1 (bullet) and Q2 (cartridge) for comparison. They still hadn't arrived however, something that could indicate he had lost control of the investigation, and accident or not, this mistake could have helped force his departure.

Stanley Zaverl was immediately appointed as the new acting chief of police, and on December 7 it was Wirth who finally sent Q1 and Q2 to the

FBI, along with a bullet and cartridge from a Hi Standard Model G .380 semi-automatic pistol (serial number 1154 or possible Gun #2, which had no details about where it had been obtained from).

District Attorney Ted Stevens was probably relieved that Danforth was gone, and he could start preparing for the trial of Diane and Johnny, which was scheduled for April 5, 1954. The always-crowded federal court docket was the main reason for this long delay, and since Diane was determined to get away from prying eyes, the Judge had no reason to refuse the request for her to fly to "the States" in return for another $5,000 bond. Johnny however stayed in Fairbanks for the duration.

Diane was now famous and infamous across America, so it might have seemed odd to some that she would head to Los Angeles. She told reporters that she was going to get treatment for "nervousness" and "a headache that aspirin doesn't help," reported *Jet*, and talking to reporters in Seattle before her connecting flight she further described the injuries she received on the night of the murder:

"I have to hide the lumps of scar tissues with these long eyebrows. That's where they hit me. I have a lump on my mouth here too."

She arrived in the smog of L.A. on December 10, where overnight heavy rains and winds that caused a boulder to roll 2,000 feet down a mountain in Malibu, killing a resident in the home below, had knocked the sensational story of alleged wife murderer Dr. Samuel Sheppard off the front page of the *Los Angeles Times*. Diane's arrival wasn't reported, but the *Sitka Sentinel* noted that she had a more obvious reason for leaving Fairbanks: "It's cold up there, and my husband and I always came here for the winter," she said, adding that she was confident she would be acquitted:

"They haven't anything to connect me with the murder except that I was there — and beaten up terribly... the worst thing is that I'll be tried on Warren's lies, not on the facts of the case itself."

Aside from the climate and the beaches, the city had other obvious attractions. It was a glamorous place of clubs, bars, and celebrities, and, according to Saundra at least, she had already been there before, trying to find a way into the movies. Rather than couch-surfing through another harsh winter in small, gossipy Fairbanks, this seemed an obvious choice for her and Marquam.

Perhaps more importantly, she could hope to get lost among the vastness of the city's two million people.

She moved in with friends Allan and Jo Ann Mansfield, who lived in Baldwin Hills in the south of the city. Jo Ann was also described as an "attractive blonde" in her 30s, and she told reporters that she and her husband had first met the Wellses in South America.

Another one of those friends was William Colombany, who had closed his dance school and moved to Los Angeles soon after Diane left, according to the *FDNM*, and was now living there with his mother Rebecca and sister Marina. He was on hand to enroll young Marquam in a nursery school, and it seemed that he and the Mansfields wanted to try and keep life as normal as possible for Diane — at least until the trial.

But she just couldn't escape the investigation.

As the temperature plummeted towards minus 30 in Fairbanks, on December 12 there was a possible break in the case.

Among the 24 cartridges sent from the .380 Italian Beretta (possible Gun #1), a single match had been made with the Q2 cartridge: they had identical markings on the brass case which "could have been produced by the lips of the same clip." There was also an ejector mark on the head of one of the other cartridges, though that identification was limited, but there was no connection at all to possible Gun #2, the Hi Standard Model G .380 semi-automatic pistol.

A few days later, US Marshal Dorsh finally sent the FBI something that should have been in the original boxes of evidence: the replacement green-and-white striped pajamas Diane was wearing the night Cecil was shot. Belatedly coded as Q15, they featured a design of circles with a horse and rider, and were bought at the City of Paris store in San Francisco. Dorsh asked for the bloodstain on them to be analyzed, and whether there were any powder burns on the sleeves:

"Does it look as though blood may have sprayed back on either sleeve from the shot. That is if she did shoot him."

Depending on the circumstances GSR can last longer on clothes than it can on skin, but the report came back another two weeks later stating that there were no powder particles, residue or smudges that would permit association with a firearm.

It was the end for what could have been a major piece of evidence linking Diane to the killing, and there was never any explanation for where the pajamas had been in the two months since the murder either, though the report did mention some details about the bloodstains.

"Most of the bloodstains on the shirt portion of the Q15 pajamas appear to have been caused by drops of blood falling from the direction of the collar and proceeding towards the cuff and tail portion. The large stain on the lower right sleeve appears to be a contact stain. The relative absence of any finely splattered blood coupled with the above-mentioned directional drops indicates that the wearer was probably either a standing or a sitting position during the time the stains were deposited. No stains were found on the sleeves which would indicate that any of the blood sprayed back onto the sleeves from a person other than the wearer. The shape and appearance of the stains on the trousers are not indicative of any particular direction or manner of staining."

In other words, this matched almost exactly what Diane described: she was attacked and beaten, and blood dripped from her face and head down onto her pajamas.

As 1953 came to an end, finding the murder weapon was still the top priority for the investigation, but on January 15, 1954, the *Los Angeles* newspaper announced the marriage of Marilyn Monroe and baseball legend Joe DiMaggio, and Diane celebrated her 32nd birthday. It was meant to be a day of celebration, but both the Mansfields and Colombany had noticed warning signs of depression in Diane; she had started to lose interest in Marquam, and could only count down the days before her trial.

Then, on January 27, Colombany was arrested as a fugitive suspect in relation to Cecil's murder — though the headlines of the *Los Angeles Times* were about a robber and long-time prison escapee Alex R. Bryant, who was on the FBI's Top 10 "Most Wanted" list and was also arrested that same day.

The *Los Angeles Examiner* reported that the arrest was carried out on information received from Wirth, and we know exactly what happened because he wrote about his trip down to Los Angeles in his memoir, explaining how he teamed up with A. T. Boswell of the LAPD, a "very good, intelligent" plain clothes officer he called "Boz".

"This was like a movie!" wrote Wirth when he recalled how he and Boz followed Colombany on his bus ride home, and then almost lost track of their target. "Get out and don't lose him, I'll be right behind you!" said Boz, and Wirth wrote that he prayed "Lord, don't let me lose him!" as he followed Colombany to a smoke shop. Boz then "showed up from out of nowhere" and entered the shop as Wirth watched. Soon after Colombany came out followed by Boz, and Wirth joined him on his tail.

Once they felt they had enough evidence to pick him up they called Sylvia Kesterson, who was probably a friend or contact of Boswell's. She called Colombany to say she had a message from his dance school but couldn't tell him it over the phone, so he was to meet her at the Sideshow Bar in Hollywood.

Boz badged Colombany as soon as he arrived, and they took him to the back seat of their plain-clothes car where they quickly slipped into what Wirth wrote was the good cop/bad cop routine: Colombany asked if he could smoke and Wirth said yes, but Boz slapped the cigarette out of his hand. Colombany immediately said he knew why he was being taken in:

"You think I have something to do with this Wells murder, but I don't. In fact the day I left Fairbanks I passed a Deputy U.S. Marshal on the street and he acted as though he didn't know me."

He looked at Wirth and added "He looked a lot like you." Amazingly, it was indeed Wirth that had passed Colombany on the street, but Wirth writes that "at the time there were no mitigating circumstances by which we could hold him."

No record survives of this Hollywood arrest, and since it's standard procedure for police to look at friends and family close to the victim of a murder, perhaps this was just routine. However, the *Los Angeles Herald-Express* quoted Colombany as saying:

"I'm not talking until someone else does. There is nothing you've got on me anyway."

Routine or not, Colombany's arrest was a hammer blow for Diane. One of the few people who had stuck by her through this nightmare, who had helped her look after Marquam tried to keep her spirits up, was under suspicion too. Would this never end?

As the date for the trial got closer, the investigation ramped up its efforts to find the gun.

In February, the FBI in San Francisco reported on the "Alaskan Matter", and an exercise that must have consumed dozens of police man-hours. Acting on a request from Stevens and Wirth, the Monterey City Police Department in California contacted Still, who had registered possible Gun #1 with the Monterey Sheriff's Office, to ask if he had a bullet that they could compare with Q1.

Still explained that he had obtained the gun in Europe during WWII, but didn't have any bullets left, nor did he have the gun, which he had traded for a shotgun. The only time he thought he'd fired it was around 1947, when he was hunting wild boar in the Santa Lucia Mountains, some 20 miles outside Monterey.

Though this had been six or seven years ago, Still thought he could find the exact place on the 90,000-acre ranch where he had been hunting, and an area 100 yards by 50 yards was roped off. Then Still, the Monterey Captain, the FBI agent, four other sheriffs, a Chief of Police, another Monterey PD Captain, and a Captain and Lieutenant from the Criminal Investigation Department at Fort Ord conducted a "hands and knees" search.

Two mine detectors from Fort Ord were used, but the 11 men found nothing, not even a scrap of anything metal. How Still's former gun even came to the attention of Danforth is unknown, but now it seemed like this last, desperate attempt to link Johnny to the gun that killed Cecil had failed.

CHAPTER 19

Pulp Star

Though the trial was still a couple of months away, people could read all about the murder in the pulp magazines.

During their heyday of the 1920s and 1930s these magazines could sell a million copies per issue, and though their reign was close to an end in the 1950s, they were still extraordinarily popular. Named after the cheap wood pulp paper they were printed on, the sensational genre had its roots back in the "penny dreadfuls" of the late 19th century, and the later magazines were particularly famous for their suggestive covers of colorful illustrations and photographs.

There were many different types, most of them seeming to contain the word "Detective" in the title, but as cheap literary thrills they weren't necessarily something people collected. Many of them are all but forgotten today, though Cecil's granddaughter Cathi McMurrin told

me about an unsettling experience her father had:

"Somebody put a detective magazine in my dad's car. (It was) opened up to that page about the murder."

A prank perhaps, but at the time many people were still shocked by such lurid publications, and having a relative involved in a murder case could have been a great embarrassment.

One magazine that covered the case was the January 1954 issue of *Official Detective Stories*, which had a barely-disguised racist slur in their story entitled "Behind the Fairbanks, Alaska, Slaying — The Millionaire, the Fifth Wife, And the Drummer Boy."

The almost-cartoonish cover showed a man in top hat and tails, his white-gloved hand pointing at a black-haired woman who's lying on a red sofa rifling through a cash-filled wallet. Jewels, cash and another wallet are nearby on a table. The "millionaire" is accompanied by a policeman, his truncheon held upright in his hands and, probably not deliberately, looking very inappropriate.

On the wall behind the woman is a tattered, red Happy New Year banner, and if this was meant to represent the Wells crime it couldn't be more inaccurate, though there is a disclaimer inside: "The picture on the front cover is symbolic and does not illustrate a specific story."

Written melodramatically by Jack Heise, the piece featured another photograph of E.V. Danforth. This time he had a mustache and, wearing a fur coat and hat, he looked like a WWI flying ace.

It was this story that called Diane "the most beautiful woman in Alaska," and it breathlessly relayed the events, wondering what had happened to Cecil Wells, a "man of wealth and prominence and mystery?"

The article also mentioned that Cecil had recently had a "bitter quarrel" with a local merchant, though this man had an alibi for the murder; he had been in Seattle. The article also mentions an unnamed man who said he had seen Johnny at the Northward on the night of the murder. This man was in fact Robert Caffee, who would be heavily involved in the case later, and who was quoted as saying:

"I'm sure Johnny wouldn't be mixed up in anything. He's a pretty nice fellow. I hope I don't get him into any trouble."

Among the coy advertisements for racy novels, pseudo-love potions and less-exotic ones for back braces, dentures, hair lotions, magic tricks, small business courses and fishing lures, the March issue of *Front Page Detective* featured a small but highly evocative shot of Diane's face looking left, almost as if she's being chased.

Underneath it was the headline: "Says she'll devote her life to finding husband's killer," a quote that reminded uneasily of the vow O.J. Simpson made when he was controversially acquitted of the murders of his ex-wife Nicole and Ron Goldman in 1995.

As for the story, it was titled "Death and the Midas Touch" and was written in a newsy, gossipy tone that played very loose with some of the facts, really upped the drama, and described Diane as the mink and jewelry-draped object of desire for "most of the virile men in town."

Alaska was described as a place new to the refinements of civilization where guns are carried "as openly as Milady's purse," and in this version wily chief Danforth was the heroic cop leading from the front in what was becoming the hottest story of the year and would see revelations that were going to "sizzle like hot grease."

Apparently, when Diane had arrived at the coroner's inquest dressed in mink, the crowd on the pavement had taken a "sharp intake of breath, not unlike that accompanying the arrival of a star at a Hollywood premiere." As for Johnny, he was "quoted" later on:

"Sure I got mixed up with her, but I didn't have nothing to do with the killing. Nothing at all."

The first issue of *Five-Star Detective* came out that month too. "Too Fond of a Blonde" was the yellow-boxed headline on the cover, which had a very racy illustration of a tousle-haired, red-lipped blonde, her blue dress strap slipped off one shoulder as she seemed to be looking up from a bed.

To their many readers, these eye-catching stories were just titillating, harmless fun, not unlike what we read today in glossy celebrity-obsessed magazines, or watch go viral on social media. Unless of course you were Diane Wells, or anyone that happened to read these stories and knew her, or even passed her on the street.

Or were selected to be on the jury for her trial.

CHAPTER 20

Barbara/Doris

Los Angeles, California — February 14-March 9, 1954

After three months with the Mansfields, Diane must have felt she had outstayed her welcome. Maybe she wanted to be closer to Marquam's nursery school, or even to where Colombany was living.

A hotel would have the luxury of a private telephone line, but whatever the reason she wanted her own space, Diane was prepared to brave some of the "heaviest rains in years" (according to the *Los Angeles Times*) and checked into room 601 at the Drake Hotel on the corner of Hollywood Boulevard and N. McCadden Place on Valentine's Day, registering under the name "Barbara Walker of Seattle."

Her use of that pseudonym seemed to indicate that she didn't want to be found, but Colombany knew where she was and discreetly asked the manager to keep an eye on her. He had recently removed sleeping pills from her handbag, though he gave them back "when she calmed down."

It was reported that Diane had written to friends in Alaska saying she felt a conspiracy was underway to railroad her into a murder conviction, and she told the *Los Angeles Herald-Express* that "they don't think there is any evidence against me," and that "someone saw Johnny Warren leave our apartment house that night, but that's all there is. Still, I'm afraid the District Attorney there isn't going to let it go. It's such a big case, he's afraid to drop it."

This seems a strange thing to say when as far back as November last year Wirth had raised suspicions about a third suspect — though that was her friend Bill — but perhaps Diane was giving up hope, or knew something no one else did.

She settled into hotel life, and on March 8, Colombany took her to a matinee to "to cheer her up." He had tried to stop her reading the *Los Angeles Times* that day, because the front page told a tragic story of a three-year-old girl who had played alongside her parents all day, thinking they were "sick." In fact, her mother was dead of multiple stab wounds, while her father was severely injured: it had been a bloody murder-suicide.

Looking instead towards the bright lights of Hollywood Boulevard, glittering movie palaces like Grauman's Chinese and The Egyptian were just steps away, and that week they were showing Cold War submarine drama *Hell and High Water* and family-friendly horse drama *Gypsy Colt* respectively.

Diane and Colombany could also have walked a few blocks south to Sunset Boulevard to see the spectacle *This is Cinerama*, a documentary of thrills, performances and famous landmarks designed to show off the new widescreen process. It had been running for 11 months, and the advertisement said "You Must See It... To Believe It!"

Whichever movie they saw, Colombany walked Diane back to the Drake thinking that, at least today, she was in good spirits.

Unfortunately, that wasn't the case.

After bidding him goodnight, Diane took out a notepad and began writing in what the *Los Angeles Examiner* called "a riptide of emotion." She then put the letters in addressed envelopes and left them on the table, walked a few blocks east onto Hollywood and Vine, and at around 6.30pm she checked in at the Hollywood Plaza Hotel as "Doris May from Denver," and took the key to room 711.

At the time, the 10-storey Hollywood Plaza was a glamorous location. Almost since the day it opened in 1925, it had welcomed almost every single movie, television, music and radio star of the day. Baseball legend Babe Ruth once played ball on the roof, and "It Girl" actress Clara Bow once opened a ground floor café here. Today however, it's a retirement home for seniors.

Sometime in the small hours of the next day, she swallowed 30 barbiturate sleeping pills and began to write a note:

"Bill, I had 30 of them - 20 in my bra - I'm happy and relaxed - it was....."

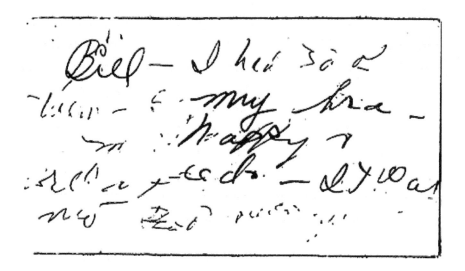

Perhaps a last-minute attempt to stop Colombany feeling guilty about giving her pills back, the writing then drifts into an unreadable scrawl. The symptoms of a barbiturates overdose would have included slow and shallow breathing, low blood pressure, possible blueness of the skin, and then eventually a loss of consciousness.

Her empty prescription bottle nearby, Diane's body was found on the floor by the chambermaid around 9.30am on Tuesday March 9. She was wearing turquoise sweater and green and black slacks, and investigating officers Detective Lieutenant A.W. Hubka and Detective Sergeant B.C. Armstrong found the letter plus $2.51 in cash, lipstick, her key from the Drake Hotel, and a green toy streetcar (perhaps a gift for Marquam?) in her purse. She was wearing her wedding ring and a gold cross necklace.

Fighting along the streets in what was an unusually windy day, the detectives made for the Drake Hotel, where they almost ran right into Colombany and Jo Ann, who had been searching for Diane after she had called Jo Ann the night before and mentioned suicide. Jo Ann had alerted the Drake Hotel manager, but by then Diane had slipped out.

In room 601 they found the three other suicide notes, the first of which was also addressed to Colombany:

Gable goble —

Thanks for being such a loyal & wonderful friend since my trouble. I mean it. And especially thanks for going out of your way so much for Mark. I won't need this on my last trip. God Bless You. — (☺ *)*

"Thanks for being such a loyal and wonderful friend during my trouble. I mean it. And especially thanks for going out of your way so much for Mark. I won't need this on my last trip. God bless you."

That penultimate line could refer to the fact she left a white St. Christopher medal with the letter, or maybe it referred to the fact her and Cecil's joint passport was among her effects. It did not, however, read like a suicide note to a lover; nor did the other one.

Another letter was to Clara Tarte:

"They can say what they wish now and I can't object. But they would have anyway. I've decided this is no worse for Mark than the terrible, widespread publicity of a trial, which is sure to crop up all his life. This will be less publicity and over sooner."

It also asked her to: "Please raise Mark as your own. He has never been baptized so it is my wish for you to have him. I would like you to have all my clothes and personal possessions which are in storage up north. God bless you, love Diane."

There was also a scrap of telephone directory held tight in her hand (or found in her handbag, depending on whether you preferred tragedy or romance). It featured the now-familiar doodle of a heart with an arrow stuck through it, and these longing words:

"Happy Valentine, I love you."

Also found in room 601 was her driving license, a business card for Allen Mansfield, and a bill for $20 from a lawyer Colombany had hired. Was Diane taking care of this bill for him, or was she the client?

Another item was a postcard dated January 22, and perhaps never sent, to someone called Sam. It said "Arrived LA today — after an overnight and a big fat steam bath at Paso Robles. After the bath and 9 hours sleep, I began to see life moving around about me. Call me at my sis' house, Sylvan 0-4664. D." In the 1950s, that phone number seemed to be for La Cañada Flintridge, California, but it remains a mystery.

There were also two photographs of blond girls, one of them standing with a dark-haired man. Perhaps it was Saundra, Bonnie, and her first husband Donald? She had carried his Bible for a number of years after their divorce, and it's not hard to imagine that she had photographs too, and took them out to look at before she decided to take her final journey.

It reminded me of the story about Grandma Lee, who kept letters from Donald reaching Saundra and her sister Bonnie. I was sure that Diane had faced the same cruelty of omission, and it became even more tragic when Saundra told me she remembered her father Donald later admitting that Diane had contacted him in early 1954, asking him to come and visit her in Hollywood.

Understandably his wife wasn't happy about this, and he refused her request — something he told Saundra that he always regretted.

Finally and perhaps most significantly, among her possessions was a *FDNM* newspaper clipping from February 25 mentioning Clyde Dailey and Wendell Henry Paust, an assistant chief of detectives and detective sergeant respectively in the Seattle Police Department.

On a conveniently-timed vacation, these "lie-detector experts" — Dailey was a graduate of the Keeler Polygraph Institute — had been hired by a representative of the Wells family to go up to Fairbanks, and had recently "tested several persons" there. Johnny's lawyer had insisted he refuse the test, but Seattle PD records later showed that the results of his test had been sent to the Fairbanks DA from San Francisco police in San Francisco in early March.

Either way, Diane would have been worried about who they had tested, and what they had said. Maybe this was the breaking point for her, but how did she get to a place where she felt that leaving Marquam an orphan was "no worse"?

Aside from the prospect of many decades in prison far away from home, she must have known that other revelations would come to light at the trial. There were her two estranged daughters for a start, and if her illegal marriage to Cecil was uncovered it would make Marquam illegitimate, and maybe put his inheritance in jeopardy.

More than anything else, the public wanted to know if Diane had written about Johnny and the murder in her final letters — and she had. Signed with her regular elaborate "D", the letter appeared confused and rambling, but seemed to finally confirm what she had always denied, and to be a confession of sorts:

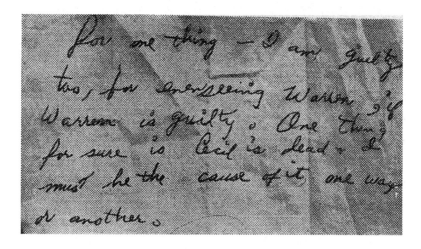

"For one thing — I am guilty too, for ever seeing Warren, if Warren is guilty. One thing for sure is Cecil is dead, and I must be the cause of it, one way or another."

Strangely, this potentially vital piece of evidence wasn't mentioned in the police report, nor was the "Happy Valentine" scrap of paper. Neither appeared in the FBI file, either.

All the newspapers, including the *FDNM*, got Diane's age wrong in their reports, and though several printed her suicide notes, only a few — including the *FDNM* — showed Diane's body, covered in a white sheet, being wheeled out of the hotel. In the background of the photograph was Colombany, with his back to the camera, and Jo Ann Mansfield. They had been sent to the Hollywood Plaza to identify the body, which was described as "still beautiful in death."

The *Los Angeles Times* headlined their front-page story "Accused Beauty Commits Suicide," while the *Los Angeles Herald-Express* headline ran "Alaska Beauty Ends Life To Help Her Young Son", and in that way at least, Diane got her wish. The story of her, Cecil and Marquam faded from the headlines quickly, but for now her suicide was a sensation — and there were still more twists to come.

DIANE WELLS KILLS SELF!

Under the *FDNM* headline "Diane Wells Kills Self!" was a "History of Diane Wells; Wed Three Times," which seemed a rather unusual angle to take, focusing on her marital relationships and absent children rather than the unhappy circumstances of her suicide. Cecil had been married five times, though that hadn't been so prominently mentioned when he died.

In the article, Jo Ann Mansfield said that Diane had become more and more despondent, and she had been worried that Diane was going to do something desperate:

"She didn't kill herself out of guilt. She felt that everyone wanted her out of the way. She was not afraid of being convicted at her trial, but she was afraid the trial would be a smear. And above all, she felt that with her out of the way, her little son would be better off."

This article featured a photograph of Jo Ann holding hands with Marquam, and she described her late friend as impractical about money, but also impulsively generous, affectionate, (and) loyal to her husband and her friends. She insisted that Diane had only met Johnny two or three times, on the advice of friends, "because she suspected he may be trying to blackmail Cecil" (perhaps with her love letters, as unlikely as that seemed).

Jo Ann added that Diane said she had slammed the door in Johnny's face when he came to the apartment insisting: "I've got to see you." Diane had told Jo Ann that she was going to confront Johnny when she got back to Fairbanks, but she had probably been in touch with him while she had been in L.A.

Diane's attorney Walter Sczudlo was far more direct about her death. Proclaiming himself shocked by the news, he told the *Daily Sitka Sentinel* that she was innocent:

"The cause of her death was malicious gossip and unfounded rumors."

Some people even had doubts that it was suicide.

"There was no way my mother killed herself," said Saundra. "She was not that kind. I do not think she took them (the barbiturates) out of her own free will. That's not her M.O. She's a survivor." Diane's ceramics teacher expressed similar sentiments, albeit in a less kind way, saying that Diane was "too conceited and self-absorbed" to take her own life.

There was less sympathy elsewhere. A 1997 letter to Jim Messer said that suicide was "a fit ending for her, I would say." A cruel comment, though it had been written by a friend of Ethel, Cecil's fourth wife. Judy Morris, Ethel's half-sister, who had gone with her husband to work close to the Canadian border during the months after the murder, recalled that she didn't feel sorry for Diane either.

Much later, I learned that the studio where Diane's grandson — Saundra's son Gary — committed suicide was very close to the Hollywood Plaza Hotel.

CHAPTER 21

A Scarlet Letter

Los Angeles, California — Wednesday March 10, 1954

A later edition of the *Los Angeles Herald-Express* had a different headline:

Beauty's Suicide May Have Been 'Too Soon'

As soon as he had heard the news, DA Stevens must have suspected this could be the end for his case. After calling Diane's death "unfortunate and tragic," he asked for the trial to be delayed, and again hinted that Johnny may not stand trial at all due to the question of prejudice, both local and racial.

He also mentioned a need for additional evidence, and I wondered if this was related to something Dailey and Paust had found out in their investigation. Interestingly, the *FDNM* report on Dailey and Paust's arrival in Fairbanks also announced Stevens' formal nomination as District Attorney by President Dwight D. Eisenhower.

Since the case was already wavering against Johnny and now the prime suspect had committed suicide, Stevens might have wanted to avoid any further negative publicity around the trial — and indeed, he was confirmed in his post soon after.

There was a flurry of letters and Western Union telegrams between Fairbanks and L.A., but while the letters Diane left behind shed some light on Cecil's murder — "I must be the cause of it, one way of another" — it was with a touch of resignation that US Marshal Dorsh wrote thanking Detective Boswell for sending the fingerprint card of Colombany.

He had been arrested and briefly questioned after Diane's suicide, but this seemed like standard procedure, especially since two of the suicide letters had been addressed to him. Dorsh wondered whether Colombany's fingerprints might match those on the whisky bottle from the crime scene, but the FBI soon confirmed that they didn't.

In return, Dorsh sent a fingerprint card of Diane to use for official identification of her body, and a few days later the report into her death was sent to Fairbanks by William H Parker, Chief of Police in Los Angeles, though Dorsh wrote back that "we hear persistent rumors of later developments."

Diane's suicide made headlines around the world, but her funeral was reported to be taking place in secret, with neither the time nor place to be revealed.

Before that could happen, her corpse had to be examined by the Los Angeles Coroner at the Hall of Justice in downtown. The building has since moved to a former hospital close to Union Station, but a deleted scene from the beginning of the classic 1950 movie *Sunset Boulevard* shows what it looked like. The layout and equipment had been the same since the 1930s, though the late 1940s did see wooden gurneys replaced with stainless steel ones as it had finally been understood that wood was porous, and not the best material for such a messy business.

It's unlikely Diane would have laid alone in room 100 that day. There were 723 suicides in Los Angeles County in 1953-1954, and 135 of them (including Diane's) listed the cause of death as "despondency."

Assistant Autopsy Surgeon Victor Cefalu examined corpse number 93284, and his report was just a single page in length. The opening paragraph noted "No external marks of violence are present," and her brain and heart were normal. Her liver and stomach contents were submitted for the presence of barbiturates and alcohol, and the chemical analysis came back the next day showing there was no ethanol (alcohol), but her liver had 9.0 mg of barbiturates per 100 grams, with amobarbital and other unidentified components present too.

Amobarbital is an odorless white powder with sedative-hypnotic properties and a slightly bitter taste, and the extreme discoloration in the prepyloric region of her stomach was an indication of the damage those barbiturates had done internally, though there were no changes in her other abdominal organs.

This tallied with the empty prescription bottle found in her room (which was made out to "Barbara"), and so it was no accidental overdose. Cefalu was quoted as saying that she had ingested enough to kill three people, but there was another observation he made that could have changed everything — and maybe it had.

Diane had been pregnant.

It began with a simple sentence: "Milky fluid exudes from the nipples of the breasts." The production of milk (actually a pre-birth substance called colostrum) begins roughly three or four months after conception, or even sooner, and can continue after an abortion or miscarriage too. The uterus was also described as "large", but the cervix was described as "irregular and somewhat hemorrhagic. No marks of instrumentation are found.... In careful search, no fetus could be found." Also, one ovary contained a corpus luteum, a collection of cells which occur during the monthly cycle and produce the hormone progesterone in anticipation of potential pregnancy.

When the abortion or miscarriage had occurred was not disclosed, but the clues were in the scientific language, and the newspapers jumped on this revelation. In summary, the autopsy indicated that Diane had recently suffered a miscarriage or undergone an "illegal operation" (the term used at the time for an abortion), or had even tried to induce one on herself.

Had this prompted her move to the privacy of the Drake Hotel? She would have known her body and whether she might be pregnant, but she would also have known what people would think when she appeared at the trial looking pregnant. If it was even suspected that the child had been fathered by Johnny, it would have been used against her. Many people would have looked down at her for having a child out of wedlock anyway, let alone with an African-American.

Alternatively, she may have become involved with someone in the last few months. An obvious candidate might be Colombany, and it could explain why he was so devoted to her. But if that affection wasn't reciprocated it could have meant more emotional complications, and wouldn't look good in the eyes of the press, the public, and especially the jury, who John Warren felt might have seen it as a "scarlet letter."

That the child might be Cecil's was a possibility too. A sympathetic jury might save her from prison if they believed she was carrying her murdered husband's child, but Alaska didn't have a dedicated women's prison. It was just as likely her newborn would be taken from her, and, according to *A Different Frontier: Criminal Justice, 1935-1965*, she would have been incarcerated at the women's prison in Alderson, West Virginia.

Acquiring an illegal operation, especially when four or five months pregnant, would have been dangerous, painful and traumatic, though there were many medical practitioners who would discreetly help with such a procedure. A search of the *Los Angeles Times* presented many examples, and one from February 28, barely two weeks before Diane's death, reported the arrest of Dr. George Davis, a 73-year-old retired osteopath, his new 36-year-old bride Nellie, and Thelma Smith, 58, a housekeeper who acted as a nurse.

The trio performed operations at the rooming house in Highland Park in northeast Los Angeles, and at a cabin in Monrovia, California. Detectives found a list of 10 previous clients, one of whom had come from over 200 miles away. Davis's fees ranged from $300-500 depending on the customer's financial circumstances. That sliding scale was a kind gesture, but it was still a lot of money, so unfortunately many ended up at less safe places.

If Diane had had an abortion there was the possibility of post-abortion grief, symptoms of which can be emotional, psychological and physical, though none of that would have been familiar to doctors at the time, let alone understood by the general public.

If she had suffered a miscarriage it would have been traumatizing too, and a 2011 paper in the *British Journal of Psychiatry* notes that even after having a healthy child, women who later miscarry can have a higher risk of postnatal depression, which reminded me of something Saundra said:

"When I was born my mother had a nervous breakdown. That tells you something. She had to be hospitalized for six or eight weeks because of that. Her health was such that she was hospitalized for six weeks at least before I was born (too)."

She explained that Diane spent that time in a nursing home in Sacramento, though it may have been for other complications to do with the pregnancy. Either way, the term "postnatal depression" was only officially recognized many decades later.

Either way, Diane went through it alone.

Her death was written up on page 284 of the LA County Coroner's Register, and at the bottom of the entry was a list of the items found on her person or in the hotel room where she had died. They included a purse and evening bag but also rings, a chain with a cross, two keys, a bracelet and three sets of earrings. Several of them had "stones" on them, and they were classified in shorthand as y.m. (seeming to be gold) and w.m. (seeming to be silver).

Since no jury or inquest was required, Diane's attorney Wallace Aiken signed for the body on behalf of Diane's mother, but it would be seven months before Diane's ashes were interred at a cemetery barely two miles from my doorstep.

I assumed that she had been buried back in Oregon, but in fact her body was transferred into the care of Utter-McKinley Mortuary, and then prepared, cremated and interred at Hollywood Memorial Park, which is now called Hollywood Forever.

Founded in 1899, it is the only cemetery actually in Hollywood, and it has a wonderful and occasionally controversial history. Located alongside Paramount Pictures Studios, who used to own an unused part of the land, the 40-acre space also operates as a music venue and filming and events location, and is a favorite for tourists.

No wonder, as it's the final resting place for celebrities including cartoon voice actor Mel Blanc, movie director Cecil B. DeMille, *King Kong* actress Fay Wray, musician and Beatle George Harrison, swashbuckling actor Douglas Fairbanks, Soundgarden rocker Chris Cornell, *Wizard of Oz* actress and singer Judy Garland, and gangster "Bugsy" Siegel.

Hollywood Forever told me that Diane's cremated remains were in the domed columbarium, the resting place for hundreds of people including Gregg Toland, the cinematographer who worked on 1941's *Citizen Kane*, and Lana Clarkson, the actress murdered by music producer Phil Spector in 2003.

Some urns stand in glass-fronted cabinets, but many more are in rows of small niches. Built in 1928, the columbarium has been developed and remodeled since then, and it has a large internal water fountain, marble floors, stained glass windows and vines and plants inside. When the sun shines through the peacock-mosaiced dome (many of these beautiful birds roam the grounds), it's an especially restful place.

Diane's marker is upstairs on the upper south wall at tier 1, niche 1. It's at floor level in a corner, and simply reads "Diane Wells 1954". Saundra and London told me they had been here when they came to collect Gary's ashes back in 2012, though neither of them recalled much about the visit.

Hollywood Forever also confirmed that Diane had been interred on Friday October 15, 1954, an unpleasantly hot, humid and smoggy day.

She had presumably been cremated soon after her death, but had her ashes then stayed on the shelf, or had someone taken them in order to organize a service? Hollywood Forever said that the first option was "much more common," and the probate records showed that it cost nearly $750 (over $7,000 today), but wasn't paid in full until over a year after her death — and it came out of her own estate.

Whatever the reason for that seven-month delay, Colombany would surely have been there for the interment, even though there was never any formal announcement of one. The Mansfields may have attended too, though it was very unlikely Marquam would have flown back from Fairbanks for it.

A few weeks before the interment, Diane's mother Florence/Yvonne had written to the LAPD in Hollywood asking who took Diane's personal belongings. They could have been collected from the coroner's office by her lawyer or friends, though it seemed this hadn't happened, and the office would have disposed of uncollected possessions after a certain period of time. As for anything the police took for evidence, that would be a different matter entirely.

More pointedly, Florence's letter asked what could be done about "who was calling her on the phone and terrifying her just prior to her death." She wrote that "Diane was driven to do what she did," and ended by saying "I am trusting you not to let anything into the hands of the press."

Was she referring to the emotional love letters that Diane sent Johnny, or those that came from so-called "well-wishers"? Under the guise of a concerned citizen, "old friend", or simply someone who wants a dash of drama in their lives, such letters are regularly sent to people jailed for scandalous or violent crimes, and Diane had a number of such letters in her possession when she died.

One dated January 18, 1954 was from a man in St. Louis, MO, who called himself "your loyal waiter." He said he hadn't heard of her in a long time, but that "smile, there's many things to say and must be said to my and your benefits," and asks her to write back so he can pass on whatever wisdom he has to offer.

Another man wrote from Anchorage on January 27 with "Confidentiality Please" underlined several times at the top. It was largely unreadable, but he was writing about something of "vital importance, and is of course something you should know before you return to Fairbanks. I will tell no one other than you," he wrote.

Some were creepier, like the neatly-written missive dated January 20 from someone at the Veteran's Hospital in Excelsior Springs, MO. Initially supportive, it slowly changes and he calls her darling, then says that he is "alone in this world," but hopes they could become "acquainted."

Why Diane kept these is hard to say: perhaps she was grateful for any kind words, even if they were from strangers.

Two more letters were from her friend and neighbor Jouida Gail, who seemed to be holding down the home front in a freezing Fairbanks. On January 28, when the temperature dipped as low as -45, she wrote "Honestly, all I could do when I received that letter was sit down and cry."

She discussed lawyer Charles Clasby, who seemed to have the keys to apartment 815 at the Northward, and said she had spent the night there when her roommate Virginia "had company." The other letter dated February 4 mentioned something that seemed to be a big problem in Fairbanks: their mutual friend William Colombany.

"Just received two letters from you today, and you really sound blue," she began. She urged Diane not to worry, and wrote that "I am sorry to know he was picked up (presumably Colombany's arrest in January). He was told over and over again not to be so obvious in running around with you for his good and yours. Everyone thinks the two of you are really carrying on. Someone is always asking me if you are engaged, married yet. So far I have received reports of the two of you being in Acapulco (honeymooning yet) and South America.... Wirth thinks you're engaged... Bill is so damned ostentatious about seeing you that they in turn think I am concealing the truth."

She suggests that Colombany should get a job as "they probably think you're supporting him too," and that she has her things "packed up, including that letter — I won't loose (sic) it, and I so appreciate you sending it to me. Damn jerks!"

It seemed like Colombany had caused a rift between them, but in fact Jouida was simply worried about how her link to a man living under a cloud of suspicion might affect her new venture: her own dance school. Jouida implores Diane to "ignore what you can and try to enjoy your stay as much as you can," and signs off saying: "Please think nice thoughts and dream sweet dreams."

Her mention of the Fairbanks gossip might relate to Florence's letter about the "terrifying" calls made to Diane at the Drake Hotel. Were journalists harassing her, or someone threatening her about what she might say at the trial?

It can't have been someone Diane knew (unless they were disguising their voice), and while the police report on her suicide noted that she had taken calls from a man stating he was her husband, the phone number of these calls (HO28183) matched that of a witness in the same report.

The "husband" and the witness were the same man: William Colombany.

Especially if calls came through a hotel switchboard, "husband" seemed an odd choice for a code word between Diane and Colombany. Had something happened that had fractured their relationship? What if Colombany had threatened to go to the police with what he knew, or said he knew? Or if she had?

Alternatively, Diane had called her ex-husband Donald in January, asking him to visit, or perhaps Johnny was disobeying his lawyer and his wife by calling her; it's easy to imagine that as the trial approached, they might have wanted to get their stories straight.

One way to make sure she never had to face any of it, to never disappoint anyone again, and to save Marquam from the chaos of a trial, was to take the barbiturates.

CHAPTER 22

Millionaire Orphan

Los Angeles, California — March 22-April 8, 1953

Cecil's will, which had been drawn up just a few months before his murder, bequeathed a monthly fund for Marquam and a two-third share of a $250,000 trust fund when he turned 22 years old. Cecil's five other children, the oldest of whom was 33, received bequests too, but Diane got the rest of his substantial assets. Reports varied wildly, but he was said to be worth around $400,000 (well over $3,750,000 today), and that figure could have been even more.

The *Anchorage Daily Times* said the estate included mining properties, equipment, buildings, stocks, shares, and bonds, and for a few months Diane had theoretically been a rich woman — something that many quickly suggested was her motive for murder. Cecil had named her as his executrix, but after her arrest that position was taken over by Reuben Tarte, and on a day-to-day basis she was short of money.

There was some income, though. Cecil's policy with Provident Life Insurance paid out over $5,000 for example, which seems to indicate that they didn't find enough evidence to deny the payment. However, Diane's lawyer Walter Sczudlo was reported as saying that Cecil was over-extended at the time of his death, and a glance at the dizzyingly-complicated 400-plus pages of his probate files show that interest charges, loans, and debts don't go away when you die.

Nor do the costs of child support, payroll, rent, storage, insurance, utilities and taxes for Cecil's businesses, the unfinished sale of their house to the

Messers, the cost of a lengthy lawsuit brought by Ethel regarding their son Wendell's share of the estate, even an outstanding laundry bill and rent for their apartment at the Northward. The list went on and on, and as inheritor, Diane was liable for all outstanding and ongoing costs.

Her own will was a much more modest affair. Written in November 1951 it bequeathed $10 each to Marquam, Saundra and Bonnie (the girls were listed as "address unknown"), and left the rest to Cecil. Now though Saundra and Bonnie were due to receive $2,500 each, while the other bequests stayed the same. Tarte was also Diane's choice as Marquam's trustee, though several other members of the Wells family were involved over the years too.

In December 1953 Diane's belongings were appraised, and the list included a diamond platinum watch, a matching aquamarine necklace, ring and earrings, and an elaborate emerald and diamond "dinner" ring. The ring alone was valued at $2,800 (over $26,000 today), and in total they were worth $8,345 (over $78,500).

Another document appraised Diane's silver blue mink jacquette and a dark ranch mink coat, possibly the one that she was photographed wearing when she came back from Seattle, at a figure of over $97,000 today.

After her suicide it all became subject to a lengthy legal battle; even the fact that she died in California but was resident in Alaska meant more paperwork and invoices. Her bill from the Drake Hotel was outstanding too.

In 1956, an inventory of the Wells estate included household furniture, fixtures and fittings, but also mining equipment, real estate lots, stocks, bonds, and mining claims. Also on the list were a "rifle in a case" and a 12 gauge shotgun, the rifle presumably the same one that police found when the searched the apartment after the murder. What happened to the target pistol they also found, and where the shotgun came from, is unknown.

The IRS wanted their cut as well, and so the coroner and the city of Los Angeles coordinated to arrange the sale of Diane's possessions at auction. On May 5, 1958 at an anonymous warehouse in downtown L.A., the auctioneer began the bidding on her wrist watch, rings, necklace, and furs — though the St. Christopher medal wasn't listed. They raised a total of $1,192.31, which was far, far less than they were worth.

Not that it really mattered. None of it ever reached her children, not even their $10, and even back in February 1955 when the coroner returned the money Diane had with her when she died, it was less the cemetery's $5 embalming fee.

In 1963 another auction was planned to sell off a set of gold-trimmed china said to be worth up to $3,000, as well as other dishes, lamps, a coffee table, vacuum cleaner and other items from the Wells' former apartment.

Cecil/Diane's probate ran all the way to December 1970, noting in the pages that the grown-up Marquam had married, had a son, got divorced, and wanted some advance monies to pay debts. Soon enough it was noted that the estate had no residue left to be distributed and was "destitute."

Even today, what happened to Cecil's estate still rankles with his children and grandchildren. Not only do they feel his murder was forgotten and unavenged, but that his hard-earned money simply disappeared over the years. "The lawyers got it all" was a term I often heard, and to them it seemed like Cecil died for nothing but memories. Cathi McMurrin expressed it even more poignantly:

"Myself and my cousin Ann, we were born nine and ten months after he died. It was like we were kind of a consolation or something."

Some of the family got some inheritance though. In an interview, Darrell Rafferty, one of Cecil's grandchildren, mentioned that Marquam bought a fishing boat, and he thought that Cecil's mother Frances received $25,000. The efforts of Cecil's eldest daughter Phyllis bought $2,000 each to her and her siblings (presumably not including Marquam) as well.

Wendell Wells' partner Sally Papandrea told me that he thought Tarte had absconded with lots of the money, and also a valuable ring belonging to Cecil. It was particularly bitter thought for Wendell, as his middle name was in honor of his father's friend and confidante, but over time he had grown to greatly dislike the connection.

We'll never know exactly what happened, but Tarte asked for payment of $3,500 in relation to his work on Cecil's estate just a few weeks after Diane died. His letter acknowledged that Diane was likely not solvent but that they should "take their chances," though his expediency was probably because he had to put up a bond of $10,000 when he was appointed as trustee.

As for the ring, that mystery can at least be solved. A document dated October 20, 1953 and signed by Tarte does acknowledge that he received Cecil's personal effects, and along with a gold wristwatch, ring of keys, a billfold of identification documents and a gold nugget — probably a good luck omen — was an "Onyx ring with diamond." It seemed to be returned to Diane though, as it was on another probate list of jewelry that belonged to her, and was valued at $500 (some $4,700 today).

Was this the wedding ring that had blood on it, but never made it into evidence? Was it sold at auction?

Either way, now that Diane was dead all those assets passed on to Marquam, and within a day or so she was all but forgotten as the newspapers focused on who was going to get custody of the newly-minted "Millionaire Orphan."

Marquam wasn't even four years old, but in barely six months he had gone from living in Fairbanks with his parents to losing his father, moving to California, losing his mother, and then being surrounded by some people he knew, and some who were strangers. He was theoretically never going to want for anything, as that $2,000 monthly fund is just shy of $18,500 today, and the two thirds of the trust fund would be worth about $1.8m, but everything had changed for him.

As a number of family members lined up to become his guardian, the public followed the story with a growing fascination. Many had read Diane's suicide letter to Clara Tarte asking her to raise Mark "as your own," and she and Reuben graciously said that they would be glad to take care of Marquam if required.

Doubtless everyone was motivated by sympathy and a real desire to care for Marquam, but the most common photograph in newspapers during this time showed him smartly-dressed in a check waistcoat and bow tie, and sitting on the lap of a lady wearing a hat and a brooch shaped like a violin. That lady was Edna Westbrook, Cecil's sister, who Clara said was "very devoted" to Marquam.

Almost immediately after Diane's death Edna's lawyer filed for temporary custody of Marquam, who was living with the Mansfields, and she immediately flew down to see her nephew. Her case was turned down, the court ruling that the Mansfields should not be compelled to give up Marquam unless they wished to do so, and they should have time to prepare a sufficient defense.

In the middle of all this, Colombany launched a wrongful arrest lawsuit against the City of Los Angeles claiming $20,000 for embarrassment and damages following his arrest back in January. He alleged that he was falsely lured from his apartment, was only released after what was described as almost 48 hours, and was given no access to an attorney. Whether the timing of this was significant, or whether he won any damages, is unknown.

A full custody hearing was set for Monday March 22, the same day that the charges against Diane were officially dropped, and many noticed that the wheels of justice were moving far quicker to determine Marquam's fate than they ever did for his late father. As for his mother's death, the *Seattle Times* reported that he was considered too young to be told about it, while the Los Angeles Times said Marquam was "still not realizing his mother is dead."

Edna had a strong case. She was nominated as guardian in both Cecil and Diane's wills, and in the *Los Angeles Examiner* she was reported as saying that "the little boy is going to be a great comfort to us now that he (Cecil) is gone. He was taking Cecil's place in my heart after Cecil's death. I tried to be a mother to Diane too, but she wouldn't let me." It was a comment that gave some context to Diane's suicide note about the Tartes taking Marquam, but would a court agree to the scribbled wishes of a dying woman?

Diane's mother Florence was also listed on the petition for custody, as was Clayton Wells, Cecil's eldest son, and the group met at Hollywood Police Station. An attorney represented Florence, and Detective A.W. Hubka, who investigated Diane's suicide, addressed them all.

It was reportedly a peaceful and co-operative meeting, and a joint statement was issued saying everyone wanted what was best for the child, and that no one wanted to make a lawsuit or fight out of the situation. Sure enough, a legal battle began, and the *Los Angeles Times* referred to Marquam as "the prize."

A week later, people were reading about it in Australia when *The Truth* ran an article called "The Blonde Beauty and the Black Drummer" in their Sunday magazine. It featured the now-familiar head shot of Diane and a new photograph of a cheeky-looking Marquam, but also, rather tastelessly, it had an illustration of a glass of water surrounded by pills. It told how "the tormented widow passed sentence on herself," her intimacy with "negro" Johnny, and the battle over "poor-little-rich" Marquam with his "prominent, little boy ears" in a "grim story of lovers, murderers and a little boy lost."

Back in Los Angeles, the court saw Florence becoming emotional when she took the stand. She was probably wondering whether she would ever see Marquam again, and testified that she feared for him in a small town like Fairbanks:

"Things that would be said would make his life very difficult there. But here, in a large city, he could be shielded from such hurt."

When she was asked whether she wanted to care for Marquam, she began crying and replied:

"Oh yes sir, I do!"

Even though the Mansfields had become close to Marquam they didn't join the petition, though they did testify that Diane had said she and Marquam planned to live in Los Angeles if she was cleared of the murder charge. The Tartes however said the opposite, insisting that Diane was going to leave Marquam with them in Seattle during the trial, and then live with him there if she was set free.

Nevertheless, the Judge felt that Edna's younger age (she was 46, Florence was 56), was a factor. Also, Edna had been left $2,000 by Cecil in his will, had already raised four children, and enjoyed an excellent reputation in Fairbanks. Florence, the *Daily Sitka Sentinel* felt it necessary to mention, was twice-divorced.

On Thursday April 8, Edna was awarded custody of Marquam, and it was reported that he was immediately being taken back to Fairbanks. The *FDNM* ran the story on its front page, while there was a six-page special supplement about the fight for Statehood; maybe there was a hope that the Cecil Wells murder case could now be quietly forgotten.

As for Marquam's time living with Edna and her husband Clarence, that was hard to find out much about. I was told that young Marquam had also been looked after by Cecil's brother Max and his wife, but it had been an unhappy period, and he had "despised" them.

At least he didn't see the cruel headline in the *Oakland Tribune* on March 10:

Aunt to Take Murder Orphan

CHAPTER 23

Searching for Marquam

So what had happened to Marquam after he went back to Fairbanks, and during all the years since then?

For almost everyone, especially the public, he was frozen in black and white photographs at three and a half years old, his childhood tied to his financial worth. Many readers probably never gave him another thought. After all, he was left lots of money by his father, so surely he had no worries?

Despite his unusual name — Marquam Lathrop (Wells) — there was nothing online about him. The only lead came from a now-deleted crime-related discussion group, and it turned out to be my first contact with Bonnie Walker, Diane's second daughter. However, at the time her son — Diane's grandson — warned me off, as it seemed that other people had contacted her before, and it had been an unhappy experience. Luckily, when I contacted her again after I had spoken to Saundra and several Wells family members, she was pleased to talk.

At that stage though, I was no nearer to learning about Marquam's life.

Several of his half-siblings were more than 25 years older than him, and had families of their own when he was born, which might explain the lack of a strong connection. Cecil Junior (13) and Wendell (7 ½) might have spent more time with their new baby brother, but Cecil Junior told me he hadn't heard anything about him since 1952.

Mary Lou Halvorson was one of Reuben and Clara Tarte's children, and her husband Byron and she remembered when Marquam spent two months with their family after the murder, a fact that was also mentioned by Karin Wells (no relation), a granddaughter of the Tartes. Byron said Marquam was "highly strung, always moving around." He always managed to escape his crib, and once he managed to scratch a mirror with a nail file, while another time he filled the toilet with all the toilet paper.

Mary Lou and her sister Teresa often got stuck "babysitting" Marquam, and considered him rather a handful, but felt that he still didn't know what had happened to his parents, in part because "in those years people didn't talk about that kind of thing. That kind of thing was kind of hush-hush."

Darrell Rafferty was barely a teenager at the time of the murder, but he knew Marquam "until he was roughly about 8 or 9 years old. He was kind of a brattish child. After his parents' death he didn't turn out very well." He posted several snapshots on Facebook that were dated 1951 and showed a tinseled Christmas tree, parents, and pajama-clad children with unwrapped gifts. It's a chaotic, fun scene, and in a couple of the snapshots are Diane, Cecil and "nephew Marquam."

He added that later in life Marquam had "hit Phyllis up for a couple of loans. It was a sad point for her. Of course she gave it to him. It was one way to get rid of him that he would disappear and not come back. The last we heard he'd gone to prison… and none of the people I know have had any contact with him in years and years and years."

He was however able to explain the choice of "Lathrop" as Marquam's middle name, which he thinks was probably chosen "to show off." Austin "Cap" Lathrop had been the richest man in Alaska, with interests in mining, oil, radio, television and movie theaters across the territory.

At one time he owned the *Fairbanks Daily News-Miner*, though his biggest scheme was the 1924 adventure-drama *The Chechahcos*, a 12-reel movie which, for the first time, was to be partly shot on frozen rivers and a glacier actually in Alaska. Despite a successful screening at the White House, the melodramatic Gold Rush story was a flop.

The character of businessman Zeb Kennedy in the 1958 Edna Ferber novel *Ice Palace* was also said to be based on Lathrop, and the 1960 movie adaptation briefly featured the Northward Building, which was the home of Kennedy (played by Richard Burton). Despite it being a box office dud, posters for it are still proudly displayed in the lobby, and many locals still call it "The Ice Palace."

As for Lathrop, it's likely he was aware of Cecil and his business interests, even if they never actually met. The choice may have been a tribute, as Lathrop died in an accident at one of his coal plants in July 1950, just a few weeks before Marquam was born.

Tribute or not it showed that Cecil had high hopes for his newborn son, but at this point I didn't even know if Marquam was dead or alive — and there was only one person named Marq Wells on Facebook.

A native of Apple Valley, Minnesota, Marq, who never uses the "Junior" suffix, is married to Rona, and they have a teenage daughter named Kacee:

"She's getting to that age when she asks me about my father and my grandfather, and I don't really know what to tell her."

He sent me a snapshot of Kacee, and asked if she looked like Diane. I asked if he had any of his father too, but he replied:

"I don't have anything but a side shot from when he was 19 or so. He didn't allow me to take any pictures when I left home."

I later learned that Saundra didn't have any snapshots of Marquam as an adult either, but through Marq I was able to learn that Marquam had been married several times, and had another son named Jody, but after that the trail went cold.

Marq hadn't been in touch with his father for over 35 years, and had also had a difficult childhood and early adult life.

However, in the last few years he had wondered if his father might want to get in touch, which was why he had changed his name from Mark back to Marq on social media; he had changed it originally because his father's credit history had become entangled with his:

"I didn't do it to be cutesy or anything like that. I just ... I wanted ... if somebody did want to find me, I thought it would be a pretty big clue that that's the right guy, you know? I wasn't hiding, you know? But for years, I didn't want to have any association with him at all. I didn't have very many good memories from my childhood concerning him."

His mother Wendy had married Marquam in Juneau on August 25, 1967, with baby Marq born a few months later on Tuesday December 26, though they divorced after just over a year together.

"Basically I have no recollection of my father until I was around seven years old," he told me, explaining that he and his mother "pretty much bopped all over the place," which meant that he spent time in some foster homes in the Anchorage area and stayed with relatives. He felt his mother got "pretty much at her wits' end when it came to raising (a child) on her own."

Marq was going to be put up for adoption, but thankfully his father agreed to take him and they returned to Fairbanks, where Marq lived until he was a teenager. The two never really got along though, something that Marq felt was due to fact that his father never had a father figure of his own.

"But I certainly wanted one," he said.

Marquam's second wife was Doris Kellogg, who he married on February 20, 1972 in Seattle. Marq recalled Doris's parents fondly, though he didn't see them after he was aged 16, in part because Marquam was often moving the family to find work. Early on he had worked for NC Machinery, analyzing oil additives that were able to handle the extreme cold in areas where they were putting the Alaska pipeline in, and there was one summer he worked away from home, and Marq stayed with a friend of a friend of the family.

At the end of that summer they moved to Washington state, but then Marquam and Doris were divorced on May 31, 1977. After the divorce Marquam took on other jobs including working as an air conditioner technician, which was where he met Trenna Jo Hill, known as "TR". They married around 1978 or 1979 and lived in Idaho, according to Marq's best estimate.

Their son Jody was named after a character in the William B. McClowsky novel *Highliners* (a story about a college kid becoming an Alaskan fisherman), but Marq hadn't seen his half-brother since he was "an adorable baby."

A real life on the Alaskan ocean was part of Marq's story too.

Soon after marrying TR, Marquam refitted a cabin cruiser into a fishing boat called the *Trenna Jo* and took it up to Alaska, where father and son spent the summer as trolling fishermen. It was apparently a success, though Marq didn't remember much other than "being bored out of my mind and pretty much miserable."

They essentially lived on the cramped boat, which didn't have any refrigeration or a home port. They would stop in at Ketchikan for supplies, but as romantic and evocative as it might seem to some, the seasonal fishing lifestyle really disrupted Marq's education and childhood:

"I probably attended ten different schools, (and) one of the problems with the fishing season is that it overlaps school by a couple months. So I was always the new kid, and it wasn't something I would wish on anyone."

Outside school, Marquam and TR decided to buy a bigger boat so that Trenna's younger daughter from a previous marriage could come along on trips. The 50-year-old luxury yacht they converted to a fishing boat was called *Nohusit*, which is Norwegian for "no house," and after getting it ship shape they went back to Alaska from Washington through British Columbia.

"And it was a beautiful trip," admitted Marq.

On his return to Fairbanks, Marq worked on another commercial fishing boat with his father, but then Marquam hit financial troubles around the same time he got divorced from TR in June 1985. Their breakup was another upheaval for Marq, who had fond memories of both TR and her parents.

"So (now) it was just him and I living in one big house, but we rarely saw each other. When I hit 15 years old I had pretty much left home anyway."

Marq went back to California to stay with his mother, but when he finished his freshman year of high school "she and I were pretty much were done. Or, you know, she couldn't handle me without a man, you know, a father figure around." At the time his iron worker stepfather Cliff was working out of state in Alaska, and, as Marq describes it, she "basically kicked me out."

So Marq traveled back up to Washington state, where he learned that the *Nohusit* had sunk and Marquam had used the insurance money to have a new boat, a fiberglass 46-footer called *Night Wing*, built in Port Angeles. "I'd been cleaning salmon and running gear since I was nine," said Marq, remembering how he anticipated another season at sea, but his father's plans for shrimp fishing, abalone diving and even a seafood company were a bust, and when he got behind on the payments for the *Night Wing* it was put up for sale.

By this time he felt like they were like brothers, rather than father and son:

"It's kind of what happens when you don't meet your son until, you know, he's seven or eight years old. There just wasn't any bonding and he had no fatherly instincts. Basically his commitment to me was to teach me how to survive."

At the time Marq was working for a pizza restaurant, and when he heard the attic room above the restaurant was available for rent, he jumped at it. Father and son were more or less emancipated from each other by now, and Marq remembers his father telling him:

"'When you come back home just make sure that your tail's between your legs.' And I remember defiantly telling him that I would only leave home once."

CHAPTER 24

An Uncomfortable Reminder

Marq only saw his father two more times:

"I was working in Kirkland, and he came by to ... I don't know why. We went and saw a movie together: Richard Pryor in *Brewster's Millions*. My dad was into comedies. We actually got together one other time before that when we went and saw a movie together as well."

That earlier movie was the 1984 Prince musical *Purple Rain*:

"Prince was gigantic back then, and my dad always loved music. He was probably the best influence on me in just about every way — I mean a lot of the things that I like are things that he liked. And a lot of the music I listen to is music that he listened to."

He thinks that Marquam played in a rock band in Seattle clubs at one time, and recalled a rare intimate moment they shared:

"It was one of the first conversations we ever had when I had just come to live with him. He was playing some music, and he asked me 'Do you know what the beat is?' And he was just playing, you know, different parts of the song. And you know, it helped me appreciate music more."

In different emails however, Marq described him as "one of those people who, you know, is quick to crack a joke. Very charismatic, tall, attractive, and very outgoing with the right people. But then, in private, he was a different story. We got along better when he wasn't married or in a relationship, primarily because we weren't around each other very much. And it's not like I was a bad kid."

Many years later, Marq was at university when an FBI agent knocked on his door and started asking questions about his father. Marq was unable to be much help, but he did learn something important: that Marquam was living in Oregon and owned a sailboat.

Marq was reluctant to discuss his father's brushes with the law, and described them in hindsight as "something that he would use to make quick cash that he would invest into his fishing boats. So it sounds really bizarre, but I think he justified it as a means to an end-type thing." That seems to tally with the official records, which show that Marquam was on probation in Oregon. He also spent some time in prison in Arizona, but that was for other offenses in the late 1990s and early 2000s.

Looking back, Marq realizes that his father's early orphanhood had a deep effect on him.

"It certainly makes sense that that was probably what made him such a poor parent. But at the time, I just thought he was a super-mean guy. I mean, I literally would pray that every time I heard a siren, I was hoping they were coming to arrest him, and they would put me up for adoption."

On one of the few other occasions that Marquam talked about his family, he told his son that he bought a De Tomaso Pantera, a 1971 Italian sportscar, around the time he was due to inherit his trust fund, and that he had also inherited a gold mine that was apparently very lucrative, though it didn't ever seem to work out. He bought other high-end items too, though Marq added pointedly that "I'm not aware of him ever helping my mother financially."

Marquam never discussed any details of his early childhood though, and Marq feels that "over the years that I lived with him, and since, I have come to the conclusion that he doesn't have any interest in his family, perhaps including myself." Marq could only recall two meetings with extended family. Most clear was a birthday dinner for Marquam in the 1980s with Phyllis, his half-sister, and someone he thinks was called George (probably Phyllis's uncle). Marq recalled liking George, but that Phyllis "was not friendly and epitomized the, rich, stuck up, elitist type," especially after calling the restaurant they chose 'more like a dog house'."

There was a memorable moment that day though:

"My father and I posed for a photograph together, one of the only times that I remember being embraced by him in a fatherly way. I treasured the moment."

George later sent Marq Seattle Sounders soccer memorabilia and a basketball from the Seattle Supersonics basketball team, even talked about taking him to a game, "but my father's anti-family policy prevailed."

The second time was meeting Saundra (he half-recalled her nickname "Sandy"). She and her daughter Tracy stayed with them briefly, and he especially got along with Tracy. Saundra remembered this visit too, saying that it happened a few years after she and Bonnie had met Marquam for the very first time in the late 1970s.

"Bonnie wanted very badly to meet him," said Saundra, "as our Grandma Lee frequently said that she was "just like Diane," who Bon didn't know at all, and she wanted to talk to him about her. So she talked me into the trip. I was cool toward the idea, but we both went up to the state of Washington to see him. He and I hit it off immediately."

Together for the first time, she says that they talked about Cecil's murder "right away," but also visited the cabin in Hood Canal and went to see Waldo Chase, the artist Diane and Saundra had spent so many hours with years before.

On that second trip, Saundra and Tracy met TR and Marq. Marquam was working on the *Trenna Jo* at the time, but it wasn't finished. "I took another week off work as we were desperate to go to Alaska on the boat, but he didn't finish it, so we left. It prompted my then-husband to say 'I told you so'," remembered Saundra.

That visit with Phyllis and George was also the first time Marq heard any talk about Cecil's murder. It was said to be a love triangle, and he remembers thinking (or maybe he heard) that it was Diane who had caught Cecil having an affair and had shot him, and that there was no one else involved.

As the decades passed Marq worked his way through school, and has been a software developer for about 20 years.

He and his mother Wendy have a much better relationship these days, but he's still "mad" that he missed out on his grandparents. "It feels tragic at this point in my life to know so little about them," he says, yet he still talks about his father in a forgiving way:

"Despite his complete lack of parenting skills, he remains an incredibly gifted and intelligent man who at the very least answered the call of fatherhood on that fateful day my mother threatened to put me up for adoption."

Despite Marq's hopes, no letter, phone call or email has ever come from his father, though he gave me Marquam's last known address at the Oregon marina, and the boat name *Aleta* (which means "fin" or "flipper"), which he had found a snapshot of. When boats are sold the new owner often changes the name, but when I checked marine records I found that the *Aleta* was still moored there, so I called the harbor master and left a message.

Less than half an hour later my phone rang. It was Marquam Wells, and we spoke for about half an hour.

Firstly, he said that some of the newspaper photographs around the time of the custody battle were as staged as those taken in Fisher's Studio. He particularly remembered one of him with a large, black French poodle, which was captioned as happening at the Mansfields home, though Marquam said it was actually the first time he had ever seen the dog!

In almost all the photographs from that time he is smartly dressed and his hair combed, but there was another one I found which ran the day after Diane's suicide, and showed a more intimate and domestic side of mother and son. Marquam is holding a box of cereal and Diane is kneeling in front of him, her hand protectively on his hip, like they're discussing breakfast. The caption says it was taken at the Northward the previous November, just before they went down to Los Angeles.

Another joyful moment during a studio portrait session shows Marquam grabbing at his mother's necklace, only this time his hair is not flattened and straight, but a loose mop of blond curls that exactly matches her thicker, curly hair.

Marquam talked openly and animatedly on the call, and I wrote a letter thanking him, and saying I looked forward to more conversations. He wrote back a couple of weeks later, but his letter was only two sentences long. Polite, complimentary, and to the point, it said that he didn't want to be involved any further. Like Saundra, he also called his mother "Diane."

It was bitterly disappointing, but I understood the change of heart. Marq had mentioned how his father had seemingly decided to leave his past behind, and Saundra told me that contact between them had been minimal, if at all, in the last few years. Something else she said really brought it home too:

"Mark told me that all of his life he felt like he was the uncomfortable reminder."

CHAPTER 25

Another Home Invasion

Fairbanks, Alaska — March 29, 1954-March 28, 1955

Just because Diane was dead, it didn't mean the murder investigation had ended: Johnny's name was still on the indictment.

After making bail he had stayed in Fairbanks, working at the Piggly Wiggly and playing clubs, and the American military newspaper *Stars and Stripes* reported that he had recently appeared at a charity concert, and the crowd who "braved 43 below zero weather to attend gave him a rousing hand."

Again it seemed that no one had a problem with an accused murderer working in their community, though it's not hard to imagine that just some people in that shivering crowd felt the guilty party had already paid the price for (her) crime. Fairbanks law enforcement were still determined to put together a case against Johnny though, even if the trial had just been postponed again.

They weren't the only ones still looking into the case.

Phyllis was Cecil's eldest child. She had been a welder on Liberty Ships in WWI, a firewood seller during the late Depression, and later helped her father as a gold courier. More importantly, explained her son Darrell Rafferty, she was the main conduit for keeping all branches of the family connected, and this led her to spending time and money to find out what had happened to her father.

On the other hand, Cecil's brother Max, later the mayor of Valdez, Alaska, never spoke about it. "What knowledge he might have known or maybe suspected about his brother's murder he took to his grave," Darrell told me.

Phyllis however was so unhappy with the police investigation that she spent a month in Fairbanks doing her own research. She then flew down to the Lower 48 to see someone she admired, a man called Erle Stanley Gardner, to get a recommendation from him for a private detective.

Crime fans will instantly know that name: he was an attorney and enormously successful author who wrote nearly 100 "Perry Mason" novels, many of which were adapted into radio and television programs from the 1940s to the 1960s, with regular revivals after that. The shows made actor Raymond Burr a household name, and an HBO reboot starring Welshman Matthew Rhys aired recently too.

Gardner also created *The Court of Last Resort*, a crusading project that drew on the work of his friends and contacts in the forensic, legal, investigation and law enforcement arenas. They looked to re-examine miscarriages of justice, and a 1952 book about some of the cases was made into another hit television series.

Cigar-chomping police veteran-turned-PI Glenn "Bud" Bodell was the man Gardner recommended. Bodell had helped break strikes during the building of the Hoover Dam in the 1930s, and later served as deputy coroner in Las Vegas. In March 1954, a newspaper article reported that Stevens and US Marshal Dorsh said Bodell had "one of the last letters Diane wrote to a personal friend before her death," but despite being paid a handsome fee of $5,000 (around $45,000 today), he didn't crack the case.

With police resources so often overstretched, it wasn't unusual for families and organizations in Alaska to pay for private help, and Phyllis briefly engaged the famous Pinkerton National Detective Agency too. She also contracted Wendell Paust and Clyde Dailey, the Seattle detectives who took a "vacation" to perform lie-detector duties. Paust and Dailey were involved with the case for a long time, as there were payments of $250-500 (around $2,400 to $4,800) made to them until October 1954.

Darrell also mentioned that Phyllis hired F. Lee Bailey, a lawyer with a long, colorful and controversial career. He first became famous when he helped free Sam Sheppard, a doctor convicted in 1954 of killing his wife Marilyn in circumstances that were strikingly similar to the Wells murder.

Marilyn was found beaten to death in their marital bed, and Sheppard said that he had been attacked by an unknown intruder. Then evidence of an extra-marital affair surfaced, and police began to doubt his story. After a long trial Sheppard was controversially sent to prison, but he was released in 1966 after a re-trial, thanks to the work of Bailey.

Bailey also represented "Boston Strangler" Albert DeSalvo, newspaper heiress Patty Hearst (who helped rob banks after being kidnapped by the Symbionese Liberation Army), Ernest Lou Medina, a US army captain court-martialed for the My Lai Massacre in Vietnam, and was part of O.J. Simpson's "dream team" during the sensational 1994/1995 double murder trial.

But there were no heroics this time: an email from his consultancy signed "FLB" denied any involvement.

However, on Monday March 29, Bodell would have been on high alert — as would everyone in Fairbanks — when there was another two-man home invasion in Fairbanks.

This time it was at the residence of heating oil distributor and car rental agency owner George Nehrbas, and saw the men force their way through the front door around 10pm the night before. The temperature was barely in the 20s, which partly explained why both men wore gloves and had mufflers over their faces, and Nehrbas said one was 5 ft 8, dressed in a cab driver uniform of brown overalls and a cap and carrying an empty "package," while the other was 5ft 11. He told police that one of the men went straight down into the basement to his safe, but on finding that it only contained $100 he declared:

"There's been two prominent businessmen killed in this town. Tommy Wright and Cecil Wells. You are going to be next."

This "bandit" then threatened to kill Mrs. Nehrbas if he wasn't driven to the office safe, but settled for ransacking the house. Taking a slug from a quart of whisky, they rifled through Mrs. Nehrbas's purse and took two of her diamond rings, then $300 cash from Nehrbas. They unplugged the phone and told the frightened couple not to call the police, then half-heartedly apologized that they had been "misinformed" before fleeing into the night.

Following Wright and Wells (and Hausmann before that too), this was now the fourth attack with the same or similar modus operandi, and the

FDNM reported that police were looking at them as being connected. They also speculated that the criminals took such care to avoid being identified because their faces might have been known to their victims. The next day, an editorial mentioned the Wells family had engaged a private detective, and said that these crimes were "morally and economically damaging to Fairbanks," and urged the hiring of "an outstanding man" to direct detective work in the city.

Perhaps Diane's story about ruthless thieves had been true after all — though it was too late for her now.

Spurred into action, on April 16 the US Marshal's Office in Fairbanks sent yet more bullets and cartridges fired from a .380 Italian Beretta (serial number 976578 or possible Gun #3), to the FBI. Again, the source for the gun wasn't noted, and again there was no connection to Q1 or Q2.

Three months later, Wirth requested the kickback sheets (criminal records) on Howard James "Pete" Lloyd and Travis Oral Spaulding. Neither of them had been arrested in Fairbanks before Cecil's murder, but it didn't matter anyway, as neither of their fingerprints matched the ones found on the whiskey bottle.

For nine long months, the Cecil Wells murder case went cold.

Then on Monday March 28, 1955 there was definite news of a trial, only it wasn't against Johnny.

COLOMBANY INDICTED IN WELLS CASE; PERJURY CHARGE LODGED

Perjury is the intentional act of swearing a false oath or falsifying an affirmation to tell the truth, either spoken or written, concerning matters related to an official proceeding. Specifically, it was alleged that Colombany had asked Robert Caffee to testify falsely against Johnny Warren, and to "take the heat off" Diane when the trial had been approaching in 1954.

But that trial had never happened, and Diane had been dead for over a year, so why did DA Stevens want to bring this to court? Even with Wirth's suspicions about him being the "third suspect", what did it matter what Colombany said or didn't say, even if Johnny was — barely — still on the hook?

The charges had been in the planning for a while. A secret indictment had been issued by the grand jury in January, and on March 14 Detective Boswell, who would have been a familiar face to Colombany by then, again arrested him in Los Angeles.

One of Colombany's attorneys, Mildred Lanore Gilmore, flew up to Fairbanks from Los Angeles to fight his corner. A former juvenile probation officer, she already knew about being in the spotlight as she had appeared on television game show "What's My Line?" as the rare female owner of a private detective agency. She was a no-nonsense firebrand, and she soon became a talking point in Fairbanks.

Gilmore revealed to reporters that Caffee had once worked at the Talk of the Town, though he was currently employed on as a camp manager on the 626-mile-long Haines-Fairbanks pipeline being built in the Yukon Territory. Star witness he was though, and the sum of just over $359 (nearly $3,400 today) was paid for his "Subsistence, Waiting Time and Mileage" expenses.

Colombany was free on a $3,000 bond, but Gilmore argued that he wasn't a flight risk as he had visited Nicaragua several times recently, and returned of his own free will. In "stormy sessions" with Stevens, Gilmore refused to let Colombany take a lie detector test, and vowed to fight his extradition to Alaska.

Preparing to fly back to California, she snapped at reporters that her client was "the last pigeon that the police have in this case," and that she was "convinced that Fairbanks authorities are trying to hang something on him."

Gilmore's fire only burned briefly. Unknown to her, the extradition order had already been approved, and the April 4 edition of the *FDNM* showed a photograph of Colombany accompanied by Boswell and a Los Angeles US Deputy Marshal stepping off the plane back in Fairbanks.

Boswell and Stevens spoke about the extradition several weeks earlier, and Boswell asked:

"Without being quoted, have you got a pretty good chance of sticking the guy on this, do you think?"

Stevens shrewdly replied that it depends, and Boswell described how the LAPD had been watching Colombany at his mother's residence. It doesn't seem like they were talking about a suspect facing a simple perjury charge.

Flying to Fairbanks from L.A. involves a connecting flight from Seattle, and it's possible that Colombany was photographed by the police there if a temporary jail stay or a lie detector test took place during the extradition journey. Dailey and Paust were based in Seattle of course, and this time they might have been on official police business because a Seattle-labeled mugshot of a man assigned number 37433 or 37422 was found in Wirth's papers.

"Suspect in the Wells case" was written on the back, and it looked very much like William Colombany.

Colombany was arraigned at the Federal Building, and given bail of $5,000 with another $5,000 if he wished to leave the territory. The bond wasn't posted, and Colombany's young lawyer Eugene V. Miller argued that the case should be dismissed, since the alleged perjury was said to have happened on November 1, 1953, two days before the indictment was even brought against Johnny and Diane. How could Colombany be charged with trying to influence a murder case that hadn't been legally defined as one?

The *Compiled Laws of the Territory of Alaska* disagreed. As long as the alleged offense happened within three years from the date the perjury indictment was issued, it was valid. The defense also took a hit when they argued that Caffee's evidence needed corroboration from another witness. In fact, all the Government had to do was prove its case beyond reasonable doubt.

CHAPTER 26

The Third Suspect

Colombany remained in jail thanks to a full court calendar, with case number 1994 not starting until Wednesday April 20, when he entered his plea of "Not Guilty" to Judge Vernon D. Forbes. Watching from the gallery were members of the Wells family and Cecil's business associates as, finally, nine men and three women were chosen for jury duty.

Stevens and George M. Yeager, a young assistant US Attorney, were prosecuting the case, while Colombany was represented by Miller and Warren Taylor, plus the returned Mildred Gilmore and a mysterious "Miss Anderson." The next day the *FDNM* revealed more about the bespectacled Anderson, who was described as Colombany's "recent jail visitor" and "interested court room spectator."

Her full name was Kathleen Elizabeth Anderson McAfee, and she was the wife of Las Vegas resort owner Guy McAfee. A former firefighter and vice squad detective, he had moved into owning brothels and saloons in L.A., but in 1938 he left for Nevada, where he played a pivotal role in some of the early casinos. He was involved with the Stardust at one time, ran the Golden Nugget Casino from 1952-1960, and it's said he coined the name "the Las Vegas Strip" after the Sunset Strip he had left behind.

Kathleen was some 21 years younger than her husband, and they lived with their adopted daughter in Beverly Hills, though they also had an apartment at the Biltmore Hotel in downtown Los Angeles. Their Vegas base was at the El Rancho Hotel and Casino, which McAfee also managed.

Quite why an ex-showgirl with a mobster-connected husband was sitting at the defense table wasn't clear, as she certainly wasn't a lawyer.

During the trial, Caffee testified that he had known Colombany since 1950, when he rented a dance studio room from him in Anchorage, plus Colombany was also the manager/co-owner of the Ambassador Club where Caffee had sometimes worked. In Fairbanks, Caffee had once worked at Island Home Realty, showing off their model homes during the day, but at night he was known as Bob "Go To" Caffee when he played the drums at the Talk of the Town. He met Johnny the day he arrived in town in 1952, had bought a set of drums from him for $125, and also knew him via the Musician's Union.

Caffee also knew Diane Wells, though it was in rather a creepy way. He lived in the Northward in room 819, and his window was opposite the Wells'. In April 1953 he, Colombany and two other friends were together in his apartment drinking and looking across — maybe even voyeuristically peeping — at Diane. They discussed "how it would be very nice for somebody to get next to her," something Caffee dismissed as "just general talk that fellows have when they get together and start discussing a woman."

His behavior towards Diane was mentioned again later, because after the burglary/murder he had sent her some flowers, and some wondered whether he had a little crush on her. Colombany said that sending flowers was improper, though he himself had visited Diane at the hospital and her various accommodations in the days and weeks after the murder. Was he jealous?

Caffee also admitted that Diane had come to his real estate office several times, and that they had had cocktails and "drove round a couple of times." This was probably true, as in 1952 the Wellses were selling their house in Garden Island, and looking for somewhere new to live.

It quickly seemed that Stevens wasn't focusing on what Colombany had allegedly said to subvert the trial but, as Chuck Hoyt reported in the *FDNM*, to publicly investigate Cecil's murder, and Johnny's possible involvement in it.

Caffee testified that he believed Johnny had left town the night of the murder, though this wasn't in dispute. Johnny had told him his mother was suffering from cancer and he was planning to visit her, something he needed money for, hence the selling of his drum set. Caffee was to meet Johnny at the Talk of the Town on the night of October 16/17 to give him the last $50 payment on the drums, but Johnny never showed so he gave the money to Clara, Johnny's wife, a week later.

After Diane and Johnny had been indicted, Caffee said Colombany gave him a story to tell: that Johnny had asked him how he could get to "know" Diane (as he knew she was his neighbor in the Northward), and that Johnny had asked Colombany the same question. However, Caffee was then to say that Johnny had backed off and told him to forget it as "they were getting pretty hot on his trail… and he didn't want to become involved… he was afraid her husband was after him, and that he was going to leave town."

It was suggested that Colombany wanted to take the pressure off Diane, perhaps by using Caffee to plant the idea that Cecil had found out about the affair, or was becoming suspicious, and that maybe there had been a confrontation between husband and lover, rather than a deadly row between husband and wife?

Caffee told Colombany he didn't want to get involved: if Johnny was guilty, then why did he need to say anything at all? Colombany pressed harder, saying that Diane had spoken to him about Johnny's guilt, and had written a letter to Johnny about it. That letter was now in the possession of the authorities. If that was true, asked Caffee, then why did he need to say anything?

Colombany seemed to think that if the public didn't believe in the affair, then they might be persuaded to see Diane as a victim of the home invasion, and of the unwanted attention of a "negro" musician. He "wanted to take the spotlight off it" and to "take the strain away from her," said Caffee, who feared that Colombany might not be working alone when he was promised that "people" would take care of him if he cooperated, but he'd face harm if he didn't go along with the plan.

Much time was taken up discussing this alleged letter, which Wirth then produced in court. Colombany's lawyer Taylor queried whether the focus shouldn't stay on the perjury charge, and the judge asked whether the letter was addressed to Colombany, which it wasn't. However, Stevens persisted that if the letter did indeed indicate Johnny's guilt, then Colombany's pressuring of Caffee had some basis in truth.

Overall it seemed like Stevens was using a little showmanship to prove he was still pursuing the Wells murder case. Getting the letter introduced into evidence, maybe even having it read aloud, meant it could be used against Johnny later on. His plan failed, though he did get to ask Wirth whether Johnny was the moving party in the affair, and in the death of Cecil.

As for the letter, it was announced as being postmarked September 28, 1953, which meant that it was the letter Diane sent to Johnny containing the charmingly lovesick poem — and nothing about the murder. The FBI had proved that the handwriting in it was Diane's by then, so it was easy to see why Stevens wanted it made public.

Regardless of that, Caffee wasn't even an impressive witness for the prosecution.

He was frequently wrong about the day Cecil was murdered, and couldn't remember his wedding date (even though he'd only been married a couple of years, and had a daughter). Ironically, the only date he was sure of was November 17, 1953, as that was the day he got served with divorce papers!

Colombany's lawyer Warren Taylor also brought to light that there had been bad blood between him and Colombany back in Anchorage. Apparently Caffee had stepped in when Colombany was "slapping around" his wife Florence Rae Bailey after a row. She called the police, and Colombany had to pay $100 bail to get out of jail. There was a public verbal row between Caffee and Colombany at a cocktail bar too, and Taylor coyly suggested that perhaps Caffee had come up this scheme himself: maybe he wanted to ensure Diane remained a free woman, and a very rich widow?

Wirth also sounded the alarm about Caffee. He told the court that he and Danforth had interrogated him several times, and thought he could have been the man who bought the gun off Johnny at the Talk of the Town, and that he might have been one of the two men heard running on the stairs on the night of the murder.

Caffee realized with a shock that he now had some real skin in the game, especially when he was asked:

"Is murder an everyday occurrence in your life, Mr. Caffee?"

CHAPTER 27

Filet mignon in L.A.

Finally, Colombany took his place on the stand.

Dressed smartly with a lick of black hair and thick black glasses, he looked somewhat like Roy Orbison. The transcript showed that he spoke with a clipped accent, English not being his mother tongue, and at times it seemed like he was struggling to understand what he was being asked.

He admitted to seeing and talking to Caffee many times at the Talk of The Town, even to discussing the Cecil Wells murder with him, but vigorously denied asking him to make any untrue statements — though that wasn't what he was mainly questioned about.

He explained that he first came to Fairbanks in 1952 and moved there permanently around March 1953, when his first job was as a bartender. He left in November or early December that year to go and see his mother in Los Angeles, and during his time there he was hired to work on several fruitless prospecting trips looking for "radioactive materials, atomic energy" in Columbia, Mexico and, four times, in Guatemala.

He didn't mention that he left for L.A. about the same time Diane and Marquam moved there too.

He was also rather hesitant to talk about the stag-heavy night in Caffee's apartment, but added that Caffee said he had been in Diane's apartment that same night, and she to his, earlier that evening. That was probably just wishful thinking on Caffee's part, but Colombany said he did remember Caffee saying he was interested in Diane.

On the stand, Colombany came across as good mannered, shy, and perhaps a kind but platonic friend with a shoulder for Diane to cry on. You can almost imagine him blushing when he met her in the Northward elevator or lobby after that boozy night, but of course he could have exaggerated that effect in court and, if his many South American trips were anything to go by, he surely wasn't short of confidence.

Colombany also explained that he first met Johnny at the Fairbanks Country Club a few months after he first arrived in town, and that they were business acquaintances rather than friends. He also said that he saw Johnny and Caffee talking at the bandstand in the Talk of The Town at around 1.30am on the night of the murder. He recalled the moment exactly because Johnny was saying goodbye to his friends (before leaving town), and had been due to play at an event he was organizing:

"I thought there goes my music, have to get me another drummer."

Earlier, Caffee had testified that Johnny never showed that night, but Colombany mentioned a number of other witnesses including the hat-check girl and a bartender from the Player's Club who had also seen him there.

However, Colombany had some discrepancies on record too.

In the police report of the Wells murder, he said he had been at The Talk of the Town with friend Louis Krize and others until around 4am, but now his story changed. Now he said that Krize gave him a ride back from the Player's Club at around 5.30am. This was confirmed in Adele Virgin's notes of her 2002-2004 interviews with Fairbanks residents Thelma Walker and Sophie Krize, who were on a trip to Seattle when they heard about the murder. They had called home and joked:

"Can't we leave town without you guys getting into trouble?"

As for his relationship with Cecil and Diane, Colombany said they became fast friends as well as neighbors:

"I was invited to their apartment many times to have dinner with them, invited to go flying, fishing with them, invited to parties, clubs."

He added that he only went out socially with just Diane once, and cashed a check for her when she was going to Seattle.

He had become far more involved in her life after the murder, and admitted sharing "quite a few drinks" with Reuben Tarte and lawyer Wallace Aiken in L.A., and then also visiting Johnny's attorney Everett Hepp to talk about what he called "the scandal," though he denied either of these visits were to help Diane.

In January 1954 he had returned to Fairbanks for a few days, but when he heard some of the local gossip about the case, he unsuccessfully tried to see DA Stevens, something that seems to tally with Jouida Gail's exasperated letters to Diane from that time. He added that he "was close to Mrs. Wells helping her with the boy," after the murder, and that he had the key to apartment 815 and went there to "pack her things."

Stevens questioned Colombany intensely, implying that there was a jealous rivalry between him and Caffee, but Colombany denied talking to Caffee about any mysterious letter, though he admitted Diane had told him about it.

Returning to the matter of perjury, Colombany's defense was blindsided when assistant postmaster Joe Simpson testified that Colombany had also asked him to "aid" Diane with the murder charges. Simpson, who also lived in the Northward and had been on the coroner's jury, met Colombany in the elevator in the early hours of November 11, 1953.

Taylor objected, as the alleged perjury was said to have taken place on November 1, but he was overruled, and Simpson continued, saying that Colombany had told him they could "have a cup of coffee and then you can give me what information you have," before they shared drinks in his apartment. Called back to the stand, Colombany confidently explained he had simply forgotten this meeting, but admitted that they had perhaps gossiped about the Cecil Wells murder.

Quite what "aid" Simpson could have offered wasn't clear (maybe Colombany was talking about buying some of Diane's furniture?), but alongside Colombany's visits to see Diane and Johnny's lawyers, it might have swayed the jury at the last minute.

On Friday April 22, a briskly cold day, the case came to a close. The *FDNM* echoed the feeling that Cecil Wells' murder was being tried, rather than the accusation of perjury, and felt that Stevens was trying to "shake" Colombany. They also suggested that the brown-eyed, 5ft 10' defendant had something extra that could help him:

"Women jurors seem to enjoy listening to his testimony, they smile frequently at his humorous remarks, and they seem to be won over, to an extent, by his pleasant manner. There are only three men on the jury, so Colombany's fate lies largely in the hands of women."

Sexist tone aside, the newspaper thought he was going to be a free man, and just after midday the jury retired to consider its verdict.

The next day's front page had a photograph of a smiling and confident-looking Colombany. The *FDNM* reported he had been "jaunty" through the trial, and even told his jailers not to prepare dinner for him. "After the jury comes in, I'll be eating a steak in the Sports Mecca Cafe," he said, adding that "tomorrow I'll fly back to the states, and I'll be eating a filet mignon in Los Angeles this weekend."

But the headline that windy day told a very different story.

Former Dancing School Owner Shocked by Verdict of Guilty

The jury had taken barely two hours to find him guilty, and Colombany was said to be visibly shocked at the verdict. His lawyer Warren Taylor requested to poll the jurors, and they all stood to give their verdict: it was unanimous.

So much for Colombany's charm and fancy footwork.

The bewildered lawyers now turned on each other. Taylor said he was going to appeal, but Gilmore, who had kept a very low profile, said that if she had handled the case the outcome would have been different. It didn't matter now, as Colombany was facing a possible sentence of three years, and Stevens even asked for his bail to be raised, something that Judge Forbes denied.

Gilmore and Kathleen McAfee left for Los Angeles intending to seek that bail, while Caffee and the others returned to their lives. But that night in 1955 Colombany went back to the cell — and the jailers — that he was sure he'd seen for the last time. His dinner that night was, as the *FDNM* called it, "federal jail fish."

A motion for a new trial failed, and then an outright acquittal was lodged, arguing in part that Stevens' mentioning of the Colombany's arrest after the argument with Florence Rae Bailey was prejudicial, and that the evidence against him was "flimsy."

While the lawyers argued, the April 28 issue of the *FDNM* carried something startling in its "On The Inside" feature. Coming from the "Hot Tip department." It reported that Stevens was investigating sworn statements that alleged "at least two people" had been offered $10,000 and $5,000 if they would kill Wells, or arrange his death. But who had been offered that money, and who offered the bounty?

It certainly stirred some people into action, because a few days later 11 prominent Fairbanksians suddenly came together to pledge the $5,000 bond for Colombany, who was now free for the first time in weeks.

Only two names were required to be published in relation to the release of the "debonair dancer," but the *FDNM* listed all of them, and they included Lloyd Martin, Jimmy Ing, Grace Hoitt and Thelma Walker's husband Wilbur. Several of them were Northward residents, while Ing was the former owner of the Fairbanks Country Club and several bars. Ing's name would come up again later, in relation to the rumor about organized crime in Fairbanks.

It seemed that public opinion had suddenly turned in Colombany's favor, or maybe someone was worried about what he might say now he was facing prison. Perhaps he might be persuaded, or even volunteer, to tell a different story?

Meanwhile, his lawyer Warren Taylor pushed for a new trial citing newly-discovered evidence.

On May 20, Warren Brewer, the co-owner of the Talk of The Town, gave a statement to Frank Wirth swearing that he never saw Johnny talking to a very tall, blonde man (the one he said he sold his 8mm Beretta to), and that there hadn't been anyone like that in the club that night. He also said that Colombany didn't leave the club until around 4am (not the 5.30am he said on the stand), and that Colombany had been "very noticeable moving about the nightclub... as though he may have been trying to be noticeable so as to set up an alibi."

That same night, Brewer had given Caffee $50, but Johnny's wife Clara denied that Caffee had given her the $50 (the last payment for the drum set), which made him out to be a possible liar — maybe even during Colombany's trial — and it emerged that Caffee had been given a lie detector test by Dailey and Paust, with Wirth asking the questions. More importantly, if what Brewer said was true, where was the Beretta that Johnny said he had sold that night?

Another bartender at the Talk of The Town came forward to say that Johnny was at the club until at least 3am, but Stevens argued that all Wirth's new evidence was hearsay, and the motion was withdrawn.

There would be no new trial for Colombany, and now he was facing hard time –likely at McNeil Island.

A few days later the *FDNM* reported that the fire department had been called to a blaze at Colombany's apartment: had he tried to commit suicide? The answer was no; Colombany had actually discovered the fire in another apartment, and his swift action ensured there was little damage. Unsurprisingly, the manager of the Northward (and one of the 11 who had paid Colombany's bond), swore in court as a last-minute character witness for him.

Whether it made any difference or not is hard to know, but on Saturday June 18, 1955 a small article reported that early that morning Colombany had been given an 18 months sentence, suspended to just 60 days. As the locals enjoyed temperatures rising into the 70s, he came to terms with the fact that while friends could visit him in the cramped police cells at City Hall, the rations were stale bread rolls and a hot meal every other day. Sometimes the menu was supplemented by moose or caribou roadkill courtesy of the Wildlife Service — so this was going to be no picnic.

Despite the guilty verdict, many thought that the trial had been a waste of money, and in court Taylor, a long-time rival of Stevens, had accused him of grasping at straws, and alleged that he had brought the case purely to get the publicity denied him from not being able to bring Johnny and Diane to trial.

Unknown to almost everyone in the courtroom, a phone call several months earlier between Stevens and Detective Boswell in L.A. seemed to confirm exactly that.

Whether it was the same call as the transcript among Frank Wirth's papers is hard to say, but during it Stevens admitted that he didn't have enough to convict Warren, unless additional evidence was found. Most of his evidence had relied on how they could prove Diane's statements weren't true, but "now we sort of know that we will lose Warren if we go to trial, yet they (Warren's defense) are afraid if they press us to go to trial, we are liable to win."

Stevens always insisted that the Wells murder case wasn't closed, and the *FDNM* said that now Colombany was going to be "stowed away" locally he would be easy to question, but in reality, things had come to a stalemate.

When Colombany was released in August he immediately flew to Seattle, and never again returned to Fairbanks.

Frank Wirth wrote in his memoir that he couldn't imagine why Colombany got such a short prison sentence for "his part in the murder... perhaps something could be figured out by the fact that (he) was present at a large party at the home of Lloyd Martin the night he got out of jail. Judge Forbes was also at the party."

To reassure the Fairbanks public and not give any ammunition to those opposed to Alaska's bid for statehood, it could have been deemed essential that someone went to prison for Cecil's murder, even if it wasn't for the actual crime. This would have been dynamite to any newspaper at the time, and for years afterward, but it never came to light.

Decades later, almost no one knew about Colombany's conviction either, probably because it had seemed so inconsequential, and hadn't brought the killer any closer to justice.

CHAPTER 28

Exonerated

Fairbanks, Alaska — November 22, 1955-October 28, 1960

Frank Wirth, now working for the Fairbanks Police Department, hadn't given up.

A few months later in November 1955, a rusty .380 semi-automatic pistol (serial number 7243 or possible Gun #4), was sent to the FBI for testing. It had been found in the basement of the Talk of the Town, and though Wirth knew it might not even be able to be test-fired, his accompanying letter said:

"We are of the opinion that this pistol could have been the gun that fired the fatal bullet and may have been concealed in the basement of the Club since that date."

It wasn't. The return report dated December 20 said that it was a Hungarian not Italian pistol, and that the cartridges were manufactured by Remington not Western. It was a big swing and a miss, and an early Christmas present no one wanted.

That same month Clara and Johnny were divorced, though they had been living apart for some time: the 1954 Fairbanks phone book had no entry for Johnny, while Clara was listed as living at the Polaris Building. Unusually for the time, Johnny was awarded custody of their adopted daughter Susanna. Clara was to have reasonable rights of visitation, and the settlement read that "an incompatibility of temperament exists... That due to opposing likes and dislikes, tastes and temperaments, there have been serious arguments and disagreements that have frustrated the purposes of matrimony." Johnny didn't contest the divorce or appear at any of the hearings, and soon after, his sister

Willia was appointed Susanna's guardian.

Trial dates for Johnny had been regularly announced — and postponed — for Johnny, and he had left Fairbanks for Oregon over a year and a half ago. Now he was back again, working the club circuit, when a January 1956 *FDNM* headline screamed "Johnny Warren To Face Trial".

DA Stevens had received information from a CI (confidential informant) that Robert Duane had been talking with Johnny in the lobby of the Northward on the night of the murder, and he wanted to issue a subpoena for him. Though Duane's name was heavily redacted in the FBI file, it was possible to tell from an earlier report that the CI was Duane's ex-wife, but both she and a gym owner friend hadn't seen Duane since late 1953, when he had left Fairbanks in a hurry after passing a bad check.

With Johnny's trial set for May 21, 1956, Assistant Attorney General Warren Olney wrote to the FBI asking for assistance, and soon enough Duane was found: he was at Cook County Jail in Chicago, serving six months for obtaining money under false pretenses.

Stevens was unsure what to do. He knew that the word of an incarcerated criminal would always come under suspicion, and he was sure that Duane could use his bad check charge as leverage for his testimony. Once again the trial was postponed, the reason given being the ever-crowded schedule, but Stevens surely read that the *FDNM* had called the investigation a "comedy of errors," and this might have been the last straw for him.

Looking now to the future, in early June he resigned his post and moved to Washington, D.C. to take up a post in the Interior Department. It was a position that allowed him to push for Alaskan statehood, and was the first major step in a career that saw him serve over 41 years as the Senator from Alaska — though the Wells case was always an early stain on his reputation.

New Fairbanks DA George Yeager wouldn't give up though, and a couple of weeks later FBI Agent Francis McGinty sent a report of his interview with Duane. It showed that Duane had a photo of the Northward Building in his personal belongings, and on it the window of the Wells' apartment had been circled. He also had floor plans of the Northward and the Polaris Building.

Duane explained that this was a reply to his then-wife's relatives asking him about the murder, and that he had been drawing floor plans of the Northward and Polaris because he was thinking of opening a health club in one of them. He was less certain about why he still had the photo; perhaps he had forgotten to mail the tantalizing souvenir to his in-laws.

McGinty's report also noted that Duane had said that sometime between 2 and 6am on the morning of October 17 Johnny had told him he was acquainted with the details of Cecil's murder, and that he may also have talked about the "disposition" of the murder weapon.

Here McGinty's report however describes it as a foreign-made .32 caliber semi-automatic, not a .380 caliber or Italian Beretta. Johnny's police interview at the time mentioned he owned an antique part-.32 Cain, so was McGinty trying to connect him to another weapon? Either way, he didn't think Duane was a suspect in the murder.

The possibility of a trial had reignited interested in the case, and the July 29, 1956 edition of the *Sunday News* featured a piece called, irresistibly, "The Playgirl And the Drummer." It again placed E.V. Danforth front and center, with Stevens and Wirth ably assisting, and quoted Danforth as having said:

"Mrs. Wells did it. You can take that from me. Hold your presses. I'll have a signed confession from her."

It was a great quote, but it never happened.

It was this article that gave Johnny the amusing if exaggerated nickname "the Don Juan of the northern Wastelands," but it also mentioned Colombany as one of Diane's admirers, an allegation that rarely appeared in print, the *Pasadena Independent* in California being a rare exception. It described him as her "former boyfriend."

The *Sunday News* wrote that: "Few people actually liked Cecil. Not that anybody hated him; he was just a hard man to know." People apparently struggled to "keep track of his wives — he changed them so often," the article joked, whereas Diana (sic) indulged "in much scandalous behavior," and "entertained men at the Northward when he was out of town."

Note the use of the plural "men" in that sentence. A later paragraph, after mentioning Diane had an abortion or miscarriage shortly before she died, quoted a Fairbanks citizen as saying that "at least 10 prominent men were worried." Today we might call that slut-shaming; no wonder Diane was said to be "desperate to get out of Alaska."

Perhaps due to this prominent article, a further interview with Duane was arranged in August in Chicago. This time the report noted that Duane had worked with Johnny at the Piggly Wiggly, and they often had lunch together and socialized outside work, even after Duane was fired.

During that summer, Duane said that Warren once returned from lunch slightly intoxicated and carrying a small bottle of Scotch, and said that he had just seen his girlfriend at the Northward; apparently a blonde, white woman. Duane didn't ask for details since "Warren is a Negro," and he "felt it to be a delicate matter." He also knew that Warren was married to a white woman.

Returning to the night/morning of the murder, Duane, who was working in the shoe store at the Northward and opened up at 7am, now said he couldn't be sure whether he did or didn't see Johnny that morning, that he didn't speak to him, and only heard about the murder when a work colleague told him — though when asked, that colleague couldn't remember the conversation. Duane added that he knew nothing about the gun used in the murder, didn't own a gun himself, and never knew Johnny to own a gun.

The suddenly-forgetful Duane was led back to his cell, and that was the last time he was interviewed. McGinty's final report concluded that "no further investigation is anticipated in the immediate future."

In early 1957, the Alaska Territorial Legislature released a simple statement:

"The death penalty is and shall hereafter be abolished as punishment in Alaska for the commission of any crime."

As unlikely as the possibility of a death sentence had been, this must have been a huge relief for Johnny. The move towards statehood had helped this abolition to pass, but even after Alaska finally became the 49th State, there was one last attempt to bring Cecil's killer to justice.

On February 5, 1960 the *FDNM* reported that new Fairbanks DA William Taylor was "knee deep" in nearly 200 backed-up cases, with Johnny's the most notable of them.

A couple of weeks later, nearly six and a half years after the murder, Fairbanks' Chief of Police Stanley Zaverl asked the FBI lab to compare four more sets of fingerprints to the still-unidentified latents on the whisky bottle from the Wells crime scene.

William Colombany's were first on the list, (Zaverl may not have known his prints had been submitted before), but there was also Jack P. Martin, Douglas Joslyn and Lloyd Martin, the local businessman and Cecil's friend and business partner. Lloyd Martin was the only one of the four not to have an FBI file, and had surely visited the Wells' apartment numerous times, maybe even poured out drinks. He seemed like the biggest stretch for Zaverl, though most domestic murders do tend to be committed by someone close to the victim.

As for bartender Jack Paul Martin, who was often known as "Red," his record was clean before Cecil's murder. The Fairbanks Police Department might have been prescient though, because in 1976 he was found shot execution-style with two bullets to the back of the head. He had been the job steward on the Trans-Alaska pipeline, and his foreman had also disappeared in mysterious circumstances a few weeks earlier. Both were members of the Teamsters, a large and powerful blue-collar union with links to organized crime. They offered a $50,000 reward (close to $497,000 today) for information about Martin's murder and the still-missing foreman, but there were no takers.

Douglas Joslyn was a good potential suspect. He and his partner-in-crime had many convictions for burglary, theft, and in Joslyn's case, assault with a dangerous weapon. He "has been in and out of trouble here for the past several years" reported the *FDNM* when he was sentenced to prison on some of these charges, and it was surprising that he hadn't been looked at for Cecil's murder before this.

Perhaps inevitably, the FBI laboratory report on the quartet was only one line in length, and it confirmed there was no match with the fingerprints. Dated February 25, it was personally signed by J. Edgar Hoover without further comment.

On Friday October 28, a short Order of Dismissal saw the charges against Johnny formally dropped. There was no statute of limitations on murder, but Everett Hepp said later that Stevens "just in truth didn't have enough to bring before the courtroom," and that he was so "disgusted" at the lack of a speedy trial that he bought a motion for dismissal — and it was granted.

The decision had been made: it was over.

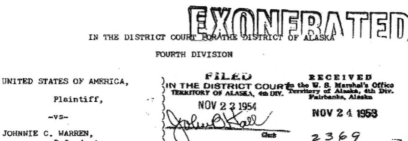

IN THE DISTRICT COURT FOR THE DISTRICT OF ALASKA

FOURTH DIVISION

UNITED STATES OF AMERICA,

      Plaintiff,

      ~vs~

JOHNNIE C. WARREN,
      Defendant.

FILED
IN THE DISTRICT COURT
TERRITORY OF ALASKA, 4th DIV.

NOV 2 3 1954

Clerk

RECEIVED
in the U. S. Marshal's Office
Territory of Alaska, 4th Div.
Fairbanks, Alaska

NOV 2 4 1953

2369

Johnnie Condon Warren was officially, finally, exonerated.

The *FDNM* didn't bother to report it, but by then Johnny was again long gone from Fairbanks. The last club advertisements mentioning him were in June 1960, so perhaps he had been on a last — farewell — tour.

I wondered how Johnny found out about the exoneration. Was it a letter in the mail, or a phone call from his lawyer? Did he celebrate that night? And then later, did he ever feel guilty about Diane's suicide, or Cecil's murder?

He did move on with his life, marrying Lillian, who was about 16 years younger than he, in Seattle in September 1964. They separated in 1975 and divorced in 1978, by which time Johnny had been living in Texas for at least six months. That September he married Ellen Mary Luce, who was 25 years old to Johnny's 59, and John Charles was born in 1981. They subsequently divorced in August 1991, but his son John said his parents remained on good terms until Johnny's death.

In his later years Johnny, a heavy smoker, had been on slow decline, and after being diagnosed with lung cancer he opted for at-home care rather than hospital treatment:

"It was actually my mother who called the paramedics to come get him. Because of him being my father, she would still have interaction involving us. Still having some love for him in a sense. It came to the point where he was a little bit incapacitated, but she would still want to check up on him."

John recalled the last few moments:

"I remember riding with him in the ambulance, and went to the hospital. The doctors said it could be a few hours, could be a few days, but it's not gonna be long. And I remember sitting by his hospital bed and bawling my eyes out and saying, 'I don't want you to leave me. I can't do this without you.' And then him telling me, saying, 'I need you to leave. I need you to go.' Because he was doing everything he could to hold on and not pass in front of me."

Half an hour after arriving home, the phone gave a "deafening" ring.

"I bolted out of the house. I ran through the neighborhood barefoot, running any ounce of emotion I could off, bawling my eyes out, and realizing that, okay, that was it. And kind of feeling really lost as a young kid, not only losing that nucleus of a family at an early age, but then losing my father and my paternal leader and advisor, if you will, at what I thought was a crucial time in a boy's age."

It was a time that led to much heart-searching for him and his mother. Since the divorce she had happily remarried, though the new relationship was a challenge for John, who entered therapy. He concluded that his stepfather was, in some ways, "a better father, a better man, just because of the things I was able to learn from him."

We speculated about what happened at the Northward Building, and I talked about my time in Fairbanks: "Still ghosts around there," he said. I mentioned that I was planning to visit Johnny's gravestone, and John told me he had chosen the epitaph and that his mother was at the service, which had a twenty-one-gun salute. He however hadn't visited in a while:

"I don't make a point to go. The one day I don't think about it, (there) always could be anything that reminds me of my dad. Could be singing in itself. Every time I sing, I kinda have that memory in the back of my mind about where I got the gift from…"

The next day at the Houston National Cemetery, I spent a few minutes enjoying the peaceful surroundings around Johnny's gravestone and left a coin on top as a sign of respect. Then it was time to leave, as cars were pulling up and a number of uninformed men carrying musical instruments had arrived; there was a canopy set up nearby, and a funeral ceremony was about to take place.

That afternoon I flew back to Los Angeles, still unable to believe that Diane's eldest daughter and Johnny's son lived just a few miles from each other.

Waiting in the mail box was a parcel.

I had tried to see if Johnny had made or played on any commercial recordings, but all I found was an undated seven-inch single that featured "I Can't Face It" written by Ray Pennington on the A side, and "Crazy" written by Willie Nelson on the flip. There was no other information available, so maybe it was a one-off studio demo by another Johnny Warren, or even came from a Voice-O-Graph, pay-operated booths popular in the 1940s, 1950s and 1960s that anyone could use for recording messages or music.

John mentioned a couple of cassettes that Johnny had recorded, though there were sadly somewhere deep in storage. He added that one of his father's favorite songs was "As Time Goes By", the romantic song written by Herman Hupfield in 1931 and made famous by Dooley Wilson when he sung it in the 1942 Humphrey Bogart/Ingrid Bergman classic *Casablanca*.

When I took the record out of its paper sleeve and turned it over to the B side, I couldn't believe my eyes.

On the label was a signature and a date, 11-20-69, and the writing style looked strangely familiar. Then I saw that the signature was spelled "Johnnie" not "Johnny".

I sent a snapshot to John, who agreed that while the "J" looked different, "the rest is consistent with others I remember." He also mentioned that Johnny wrote his middle initial "C" with a little hook, like this one, and when I examined the signatures on Johnny's marriage certificates, they tallied up convincingly.

I dug out the record player and listened (perhaps) to the voice of a man who I had never met, but knew so much about. There was no way to know for sure, and of course neither John nor his mother had heard Johnny's voice in the late 1960s, but I was pretty confident that this was indeed Johnny's "hit" single.

Soon after that, John emailed me a more recent snapshot of his father. It was the first I had seen of him since 1953/1954, but he still had that same smile, and I had been heartened to learn that John looked back fondly on his childhood.

Happy memories were rare in this story.

CHAPTER 29

Intruders

So what happened that night in October 1953?

There were several theories, and the first one related to the public statements and testimony of Diane Wells, the only witness to Cecil's murder.

She always maintained that two masked men broke into the apartment and almost immediately shot Cecil, with one of them then attacking her, and knocking her unconscious. It seemed to be a home invasion turned deadly, as a number of valuable items including jewelry and $1000 cash hidden in a desk had been taken, and Cecil's empty wallet was found in the corridor.

As for how the intruders gained access, that seemed to be via the adjoining door between 814 and 815. It was said to be permanently locked, but a photograph taken at the crime scene showed that a painting had fallen down from where it was wedged in the frame, which meant that someone had opened that door — or tried to.

There was also the frightening possibility that they had a key, or even picked the front door lock, because the risk of going to a top floor apartment seemed to indicate it had been deliberately targeted. Also, seventh floor neighbor Kathleen Walker told police that she heard what seemed like two men running down the stairway from the eighth floor around 4am, one of them saying "Oh no, no" as they ran.

There had been a number of very similar home invasions in Fairbanks. Earlier in the year Tommy Wright had been killed, and less than two weeks after the Wells murder George Nehrbas and his wife were attacked by two men, one of whom actually mentioned Wright and Wells, and threatened that George "was going to be next."

Forensic evidence partly supported her account. Two fingerprints on the whisky bottle were never identified, and then there was the undeniable fact that Diane had been badly beaten up, with the FBI's analysis of her pajamas indicating that she had bled onto them. The words from *Life* magazine were echoed again:

"Who if not thugs beat up Diane Wells so viciously?"

However, many things didn't add up in Diane's story.

For instance, she made it clear that the front door had been locked before she and Cecil went to bed, but the crime scene photographs showed there was no sign of a forced entry, and the keys for the special lock were all accounted for.

She could have accidentally left it unlocked and was too guilt-ridden to admit it, but the apartment hardly seemed ransacked, and why had the thieves not taken other expensive items, especially when they had taken the risk of going to the eighth floor when other lower floors were closer to an easier getaway? Moreover, how did they know about the table's secret compartment, let alone how to open it?

Also, how come they hit Diane with a small flowerpot (or two)? They had a gun literally to hand, or how about using their fists? No dirt from the flowers was found in Diane's hair on the scene or when she was treated at hospital, and the idea of a burglary that suddenly got out of hand was hard to believe. Cecil had been shot while he slept, rather than during a struggle or as he reached for the bedside light, let alone a possible gun, and Diane would have mentioned if she'd really fought her attackers, rather than been quickly knocked unconscious.

So who were these intruders?

The Wright, Wells and Nehrbas crimes were never solved, and only Douglas Joslyn came anywhere close to being good potential suspects. Murder would have been huge step up for them however, and only Joslyn's fingerprints were tested. They came back as no match.

Was an unknown duo of murdering thieves still on the loose? It was possible, though there were so many other potential suspects already involved in the investigation. Wirth suggested that one of them could have been Robert

Caffee, as he knew the layout of the Wells' apartment after peeping at Diane, and was also suspected of buying the gun from Johnny at the Talk of the Town. But Caffee's fingerprints weren't even tested.

Also a possibility was Robert Duane, who had the snapshot of the Wells' apartment and left town soon after the murder, but he was more of a cash conman. After interviews, FBI Agent McGinty crossed him off the list.

Then there was the favorite choice: Johnny Warren.

At six foot in height, he was a close match to the description of one of them, though Diane said she didn't notice the skin color of her attackers, something that made Danforth doubt her account even more. She "felt" her attacker was white however, which the witnesses to the Hausmann/Wright/Nehrbas crimes all said too, and while there was plenty of evidence Johnny was at the Northward, it seems absurd to think he went through the charade of putting on a disguise.

But then who was the second "intruder"? It seemed like a cover story of some kind was in place, because no one would have let two strange men into their apartment late at night, not unless they recognized or were expecting them, so it was quite possible they hadn't existed at all.

Early on in my research, I sent ex-LAPD officer Glynn Martin, a 20-year veteran with experience in vice, narcotics and anti-terrorism, several unlabeled, undated, crime scene photographs, and asked him for his thoughts.

One of his first comments was that he would "be curious to know if the lights were on when the victim was discovered."

Both Alice Orahood and Officer Templeton said the Wells' living room light was on, and it seemed reasonable that Diane had simply turned them on before the police arrived; it was still dark, around early dawn, when she said she regained consciousness and raised the alarm.

As for the bedroom, Officer Templeton said the lights were off when he arrived, and crime scene photographs showed that the curtains in that room were slightly open. Glynn explained that thieves often close the curtains and switch off the lights when they're burglarizing a property, especially at night, so that they can't be seen, but they didn't do that here. Nor did they seem to care if anyone saw a muzzle flash.

One of the two photographs showed Cecil's body, and his succinct reply to me about them first noted that the victim had sustained a single gunshot wound:

"The penetrating GSW (gunshot wound) appears to be from a medium caliber firearm, and fired from a distance, as no stippling, charring or soot are present. Rule out suicide as hand positions not consistent with entry wound, and weapon not present. No shell casings immediately present, suggesting a revolver as murder weapon."

This echoed the coroner's "burn margin" assessment of how close the gun might have been to the victim when it was fired, and Glynn added that "it appears GSW was penetrating as opposed to perforating, which means there would be an exit wound."

There had been, and investigating officers didn't immediately find the .380 cartridge or bullet at the crime scene. Glynn said that, today at least, that would be seen as a major error, as would the fact that the cause of death was initially misdiagnosed as a bludgeoning. This echoed a report in the *Pittsburgh Courier* on December 12, 1953, in which Diane hit out at the recently-resigned Danforth and what she called the "bad police work" in Fairbanks:

"He had the case all solved when he walked in… his theory went out the window when they found that my husband had been shot, not beaten to death."

The failures of the investigation were partly due to factors that still hinder law enforcement agencies today; underfunding, poor facilities, limited courtroom time, bureaucracy, inter-agency rivalry, lack of experience and training, and a small workforce. In 2019, there are just 39 full-time officers and five civilian employees at the Fairbanks Police Department.

Even so, the crime scene forensics were poorly managed from the start. Vital pieces of evidence like Cecil's bloodied wedding ring and the soiled night clothes and replacement pajamas were ignored, mislaid, or took months to get to the FBI for testing, and it all took place in the glare of the media, the grieving Wells family, and concerned locals.

Amazingly, it wasn't until 2021 before the Fairbanks Police Department hired their first CSI (Crime Scene Investigator), and she was also the first in

Alaska, too. The murder rate for Alaska that year was 8.4% per 100,000 inhabitants, placing them at number six in the list of the most dangerous states, though that was an improvement on just a couple of years earlier in 2019, when a murder occurred in Alaska every five days.

As for Johnny's confessional interview with the police in San Francisco, Glynn said that this was likely the action of someone who knew a lot about what happened, maybe even who committed the murder, but wanted to quickly make it clear he wasn't involved. Frank Wirth suggested something similar at the time, and while Johnny may have had means and opportunity, his passion for Diane was weaker than hers for him — and he knew he would immediately fall under suspicion.

But then Patty Wagner Messer told me her brother recently met an WWII veteran in a coffee shop, and the two men had reminisced about a post-war Fairbanks. The veteran remembered the Wells murder, and said that not long after it happened, he was in California and heard a "black juke joint pianist bragging about how easy it was to get away murder in Alaska." If this was true it was new evidence (albeit decades too late), though while Johnny did have a connection to California, he was still under indictment until 1960, which makes it hard to believe he would be openly boasting about it.

Either way, there were no interviews with his passengers Betty Craig or young Susanna, and two locals gave Johnny an alibi. They claimed he was at their store on Badger Road, several miles east of Fairbanks, at the time of the murder, though that depends on what time they thought the murder happened. If he was there then he wasn't close to his home, which was about a mile west of downtown. It could have been his last stop on the way out of Fairbanks.

Ultimately there just wasn't any strong physical or forensic evidence linking anyone to the alleged home invasion, let alone to Cecil's murder, and without those elements a conviction against any suspect would have been very difficult, and circumstantial at best.

Johnny's lawyers would have highlighted the fact that it seemed even perfunctory inquiries weren't made at gun and pawn shops right after the killing, and since his fingerprints weren't found at the scene, nor was he conclusively linked to the murder weapon, (which was never found), why did law enforcement still spend years and so much money chasing guns, bullets, cartridges, and unreliable witnesses?

They might also have inferred that underlying racism blinkered the investigation as it continued throughout the 1950s. *Official Detective Stories* called Johnny a "drummer boy" in its story title, and "boy" is still a derogatory and demeaning term, with an especially racist element when directed at African-American men.

Were Danforth, DA Stevens and others really so certain that they had the right woman (and man)?

On the last day of my trip to Fairbanks, Terrence Cole, the author of *Fighting for the Forty-Ninth Star*, kindly took me for beef sandwiches. We discussed the case, and he said Stevens had always felt the case was solid, and could have gone to trial, but it just never happened.

Several members of the Wells family disagreed strongly with this, and Cecil's grandson Darrell Rafferty said that "Ted Stevens just buried the crime."

Johnny may have had support from his wife, his employers, Jim Messer and the locals — and it's also hard to forget that photograph of Wirth and him, the US Marshal and the accused murderer, laughing together — but he still had to live with the fear of the death penalty, and the stress of years of trial postponements.

Then there was Diane's suicide note, which seemed to place the blame more on her than Johnny. Of all the times she could have incriminated him, that would have been it: but she didn't. In what was touted as her "last" interview, Diane told the *Los Angeles Herald-Express:*

"It's not for me to judge whether or not he's guilty. I know how it feels to be falsely accused."

CHAPTER 30

Professional Hit?

Byron Halvorson was the only person who thought Diane hired Johnny to kill Cecil, a theory that has one obvious flaw. Hitmen are usually anonymous people who stay in the background: Johnny was a popular local musician who told the police he was at the Northward, armed, on the night of the murder. Several witnesses saw him there too; not exactly the actions of a professional killer.

However, "Third Suspect" William Colombany's statements and recollections of his whereabouts the night of October 16 into October 17 were rather more scattered.

He said he had been at The Talk of the Town with friends until around 4am, a time that club manager Warren Brewer also mentioned, adding that Colombany seemed "noticeable" as he left, as if he was setting up an alibi. Jouida Gail also told police Colombany called her at around 4.30am, when he arrived back at the Northward.

During the perjury trial Colombany changed his statement, saying that he got a ride back from the Player's Club at around 5.30am, and he originally told police that he saw and heard nothing unusual when he arrived home. Dr. McLean estimated Cecil's time of death as between 5.30-6.30am, as it matched his assessment of the swelling on Diane's face. Chief of Police Danforth agreed with this assessment, as it put her squarely in the frame for the murder of her husband.

The dissenting voice was Dr. Haggland, whose autopsy concluded the time of death was earlier, between 2am and 4am, which leaves an overall timeline of roughly 3am-6am.

Colombany may simply have been a poor timekeeper, though during the perjury trial Caffee testified that Colombany threatened that "they" would "take care" of him. Also, when Colombany needed bail money his lawyer Mildred Gilmore went back to L.A. Was she going to visit Colombany's family, or did Kathleen McAfee, who supported Colombany at trial and lived with her Las Vegas mogul husband Guy in Beverly Hills, "take care" of things for her friend?

Whether the McAfee's stumped up the cash or not, Colombany was seen all over town the night of the murder, and it would take nerves of steel to be so publicly visible afterward, and then to stay so close to the case. As such, his role as a hitman can likely be discounted.

Nevertheless, when asked about Cecil's death an interviewee suggested "there was a little Mafia in the background" in relation to gambling, and Diane, scared of a return visit by the killers, reportedly hired a bodyguard within a few days of the murder. Saundra also told me that Cecil had "a lot of enemies," the *Sunday News* article in 1956 noted rumors of "dope traffic," and then there was the tip that Stevens got about bounties of $10,000 and $5,000 on Cecil's head.

Then as now, organized crime tended to work in the hidden, cash-heavy realms of prostitution, alcohol, gambling and drugs, but this was probably not a world Cecil knew well. That's not to say he was perfect, but an alleged quarrel with a merchant and a dispute with the city over a piece of land hardly seemed suspicious. He was friends with many people who had legitimate — and shady — business interests, but *Front Page Detective* wrote that he "was admittedly a man who might inspire hatred, anger or envy, but it seemed unlikely there was anyone within his orbit of either business or social acquaintanceship who would resort to murder to settle a grudge."

It was hard to see what Cecil might have done to put a target on his back, but some new and compelling evidence came from Karin Wells (no relation), who mentioned that her grandparents, Reuben and Clara Tarte, told her outright that Cecil's murder was a mob hit.

"We all knew about it. And Grandma would just get ... the older you got, the more she would let out about the mafia. I was really interested in it when

I was a kid, so I kept bugging her… and she would tell me all the stories. I wanted to know where the plates came from, and the huge vases, and stuff like that."

The Tartes seemed to have ended up with some of the Wells' household assets, including gold plates and silver, and Karin explained that after the murder, Reuben, who was involved with the administration of Cecil's will, had to go into hiding for his own protection. The situation was so dangerous that he pretended to be admitted to hospital, where police officers could stand guard outside his room:

"Cecil knew that they had put a hit out on him… and he had money stashed and all kinds of things, so he was getting all his stuff in line for Mark (Marquam), and all his possessions."

Karin never learned exactly what Cecil's connection to organized crime had been, but she said that "at the time the mafia had a big hold in Oregon which nobody knew about, and they had a guy there that did a lot of laundering of the money. And so the mob was pretty well set all up and down the west coast — even as far as Fairbanks."

Diane's home town of Portland may have seemed like a quiet city, but from around 1940-1956 it was the domain of "Big Jim" Elkins, a Texan-born bootlegger who ran the drugs, alcohol and prostitution rackets, and had an eye on gambling too. Further up the coast in Seattle, Frank Colacurcio vigorously defended his jukebox, vending machine and strip club enterprises.

In 1950, the U.S. Senate Special Committee chaired by Senator Estes Kefauver began a 15 month, country-wide investigation into organized crime. The hearings were enormously popular when they were shown on television, then a new medium, and it was the first time many people learned about organized crime in America, or even heard the term "mafia". However, the committee only spent a day in Las Vegas, and little changed as a result of its investigation — though it did make Kefauver a household name.

Neither Portland, Seattle or Alaska was mentioned in their report, though a June 1951 article in the *FDNM* nevertheless noted that organized crime was "spreading its tentacles to Alaska." $30,000 worth of heroin had been seized in Anchorage after a "vicious" crime ring had it flown it into the city, and were planning to ship or mail it to other areas.

Newspapers reported very occasional arrests for heroin possession in Fairbanks, but much more common was the influence of marijuana. "Reefers" were in circulation, the 1951 article warned, and minors especially were committing burglaries while under their smoky influence.

Anchorage was by far the biggest city in Alaska though, and it's unlikely large-scale organized crime was rushing Far North to grab a piece of the action elsewhere in the territory — at least not yet. There was money to be had though, and police officers and detectives were spread very thin (the 1950 census listed just 122 that were employed). Washington D.C. was concerned about all levels of crime though, especially in Anchorage and Fairbanks, and appeals were regularly made to Congress for more law enforcement funding. Perhaps someone had begun eyeing up Fairbanks, and Cecil had threatened to go to the police.

When I asked him about the possibility of organized crime involvement, Alaskan journalist Michael Carey suggested I check out Jimmy Ing, who had lobbied to hire a private investigator after Cecil's murder and was one of the signatories to the suddenly-appearing bond for Colombany in 1955.

Nicknamed "Robert Blue", Ing was originally from Chicago, where he spent time in Joliet Correctional Center for robbery in the 1930s, and was a bit of a showman. In November 1951 he drove around downtown Fairbanks giving out free beer as part of a price war between the city's many liquor stores, of which he owned four. He had run the Fairbanks Country Club at one time too, and a roller skating rink — which, of course, had a bar.

In the years after the murder, he was arrested for sale of illegal wholesale liquor, and for possession of a gun. In 1956 the Country Club burned to the ground, the third major blaze to hit clubs in recent months, and arson was suspected, though Ing had an alibi for that night.

A more compelling potential local suspect was the African-American Raymond Wright. "Ray" was also a local celebrity of sorts, famous for getting into trouble but somehow always avoiding jail time, probably because he was not averse to helping out the police too.

Owner of Club 69 and the Beachcomber Club, in the early 1950s alone he faced charges of assault and battery; procuring prostitution; possession and control of narcotics, and involvement in an alleged shooting at the airport in Honolulu, Hawaii. He also owed the IRS $37,000 in back taxes (over $350,000 today).

Ing, Ray and several men from Chicago were also involved in a 1956 Labor Day scam, which involved passing up to $30,000 worth of counterfeit payroll checks across Alaska. Ing dismissed all talk of Chicago hoodlums in the courtroom, but both he and Ray received long prison terms — which were reversed on Statehood in 1959. As for the money the scam obtained, that was never found (of course), and both men continued their criminal exploits to the end.

Ray was shot four times at a club in 1962 — the crime was unsolved — and Ing ended up in Reno, Nevada, where he died "in a hail of bullets" while taking loot from an art theft. An unidentified Fairbanks police officer said:

"Well, they finally got him. I couldn't think of a more fitting end."

Lastly, Frank Wirth wrote in his unpublished memoir that Lloyd Martin and Cecil Wells each had a $100,000 life insurance policy on each other. Standard business practice perhaps, but in a further draft, Wirth rewrote that sentence slightly, adding:

"Lloyd Martin got $200,000 out of those policies. Good way to go."

It would have been a big payout, but Martin had no obvious money troubles. In 1953 alone his construction company had earned several million dollars on projects at Ladd and Eielson AFBs, and there was no apparent personal animosity between the two, who were friends and business partners. Martin also had a solid alibi, as he had flown back from Seattle that morning, though his fingerprints were still sent to the FBI.

Ultimately, neither Ray Wright nor Jimmy Ing were mentioned in the FBI file, and there was no reference to organized crime or any kind of professional killing either.

As for anyone who thought Diane was the mastermind behind it all, even if she somehow had the contacts and the money to pay for a hit, she surely wouldn't have included her own bloody beating as part of the deal; the "thieves" could have just tied her hands, put on a blindfold, and locked her in a cupboard.

"She really took a hit in the media," said Cecil Wells Junior. "There were inferences, implications rather, that she was somehow complicit and so on and so forth, and perhaps she was. I will say this, I really believe that the whole thing was blown out of proportion. I think there were perhaps other people involved that had ulterior motives. (Half-brother) Wendell and I have discussed this at length, and he agrees."

If nothing else, a professional killer wouldn't have left Diane as a witness, noted Darrell Rafferty, adding wistfully:

"But in the end they didn't leave her alive, did they?"

CHAPTER 31

Mr. X the White Knight

He went to prison for perjury, but William Colombany could have been involved in Cecil's murder in a very different way, something I called the White Knight Theory.

It was the idea that Diane's first cry for help hadn't been banging on her neighbor's door, but was a phone call to someone else — or perhaps several people. Adele Virgin's interview notes revealed new evidence that Judy Morris, the person Cecil asked to befriend Diane on her arrival in Fairbanks, said Jim Messer thought Diane telephoned a Mr. X after the murder. This Mr. X made the apartment look like it had been burglarized, and, after pulling on some gloves (or just using his own fists), he gave Diane a realistic-enough beating.

This idea of a staged crime scene might explain Mrs. Van Hollebeck hearing someone say "it hurts, it hurts" around 7am, but while Colombany had been arrested in the past for hitting his then-wife Florence Rae, it's hard to believe he could manage to quietly cause such excessive injuries to his neighbor, client, and best female friend. Johnny couldn't have been Mr. X either; he had left Fairbanks hours before en route for Oakland, California, and the idea of a freelance bruiser being hired to do the punching seems even less likely.

The identity of Mr. X. was never revealed in the notes, though Messer felt that whoever he or she was, they disposed of the gun too.

Alternatively, Wirth's memoir implied that it was Sally Martin who dropped the gun into the freezing waters of the Chena River when she walked the few blocks to meet Diane at the hospital. Perhaps Diane made a call to the Martins as well?

However, the timeline was very tight for the Martins to be involved at all, even if they went to help Diane right after Sally collected Lloyd from the airport. It would also have taken some nerve for Sally, if it was indeed her, to smuggle the gun out of the apartment from under the noses of the police and medical personnel before dumping it in the river.

It could have been disposed of in a different location, at another time, and by someone else, but with the police on the hunt, keeping hold of it for any amount of time would have been a big risk, and made you a major conspirator in a cover-up — unless of course you were more than a White Knight.

Fairbanks local Thelma Walker had a "sort of" theory that Colombany had a crush on Diane ("everybody had a crush on Diane" wrote Adele Virgin), and "Bill" was certainly an extraordinarily devoted friend to Diane –especially after the murder. Before that his relationship with her may have been purely social, but either way it seemed the notoriously possessive Cecil didn't seem to consider him a threat.

Yet there was that photograph of Diane sitting in his lap, his fatherly concern for Marquam, the cautionary letters Jouida Gail wrote, his visits to Stevens, and Diane and Johnny's lawyers, and of course his illegal attempts to influence Diane's upcoming trial. They all seemed to indicate a deeper, much more complex relationship, and perhaps they had bonded over the estrangement from their respective daughters, a fact that could hardly be shared with just anyone.

Thelma also theorized that when Colombany saw Diane had been beaten up, he was so enraged that he shot Cecil.

Cecil was known to have been violent before, and Judy described him as "a wife beater" that "started slapping Diane around not long after they were married." She was an eyewitness to an earlier incident too, soon after she had first moved to Fairbanks, when she heard screaming:

"It was night, I had my pajamas on, and I ran up the stairs, threw the door open and there was Cecil slapping my sister (Ethel). At that moment, his daughter was in the room, and her mother, too. And he was still slapping my sister around."

Judy bravely wrestled Cecil off Ethel, and told him "You're not doing that again." Nevertheless, Judy liked this "charming, professional man," and said that it was only occasionally, when he was drinking, that he turned violent.

Even so, this may have led to Diane ultimately feeling trapped at home, unable to go out for fear of triggering gossip that Cecil might hear about. Judy said that Colombany was one of Diane's few friends, though she also thought that Diane "was the kind that could have an affair in a moment's notice."

Perhaps Colombany had grabbed a weapon before rushing to Diane's aid that night, or perhaps he snatched a gun from her and it was, at least for him, a crime of revenge or of passion. Alternatively, Diane could have taken Colombany's gun and used it before he could stop her.

Both scenarios might explain why he stuck so close to her after that night.

Colombany may have killed Cecil on an impulse, but what if there had been a moment when the bleeding Diane was standing before him, asking him to help her — to save her? She may have asked him to take her and Marquam away from the violence, from this cold, small-time city, and down to the bright lights of L.A.

Even if he had just helped her stage the crime scene, let alone taken on the dangerous task of spiriting away the gun, this would have been the moment any feelings he may have had would have come to the surface. Whether it was genuine or not, if she had pledged her devotion to him now that they were bonded by this dramatic moment, he might have found it impossible to resist.

Saundra told me that Diane "drew people in with her magnetism," and movies like *Double Indemnity* and *The Postman Always Rings Twice* featured women who manipulated men to do their bidding: it's perhaps no wonder she was christened "the most beautiful woman in Alaska."

Despite her insecurities and personal doubts, her public image was a glamorous one, just the way Cecil wanted and paid for it to be, and a number of men and women spoke admiringly of her good looks and fine clothes.

She had never been short of admirers, either. Donald Walker gave up high school to marry her, and a young Saundra watched her dance naked for a mysterious man. Diane also faked a wedding license so she and Cecil could marry, and when Johnny shrugged off a striptease, Diane pursued him to find out if he was the real thing. Then there were the attentions of Caffee and Duane, and so why not Colombany?

In Los Angeles he called himself her "husband," and this can only lead to one question: was there an affair, a brief liaison, or just a long flirtation between them?

Diane could have taken advantage of that, because she had the power to send him to death row. He would have to do everything she asked, whether that was taking Marquam to school, supporting her financially, or being her constant emotional companion. Over the next few months, Colombany did do all he could to keep Diane safe. There was no indication that their relationship did ever become physical, though it must have come close to crossing the line, and her hotel stay would have given them the opportunity to be alone together.

Then there was the pregnancy.

If he knew about it, and he and Diane had slept together, even just the once, he may have thought he was the father. Diane might have considered the possibility of letting him believe it, too. Marriage would probably have followed, and the *Compiled Laws of the Territory of Alaska* state that husband and wife could not be compelled to testify against each other unless they both gave their consent, or violence between them was involved.

Alternatively, if their relationship had been a platonic one, maybe Colombany would have offered to marry his pregnant friend anyway, so that she wouldn't have another child to bring up alone. Maybe love would come later, he hoped.

Either way, Diane knew how her pregnancy would look to the press, and, more importantly, to a jury. Even if she was certain Johnny (or Colombany) wasn't the father, it probably wouldn't have prevented a guilty verdict. Then she could have been facing the death penalty or, more likely, years in prison away from Marquam.

It was all too much.

She moved into the hotel, and found a way to end her pregnancy — or perhaps her body made the decision. Either way it was a traumatizing experience that she went through alone, because if Colombany as "the father" had known about it, it would have created a rift between them that could never be healed. Perhaps now she realized how much of a friend and comfort he had been to her.

As painful as it might have been, Diane could have saved Marquam and herself by saying that Colombany had killed Cecil, especially if he had done so. He had already been arrested in relation to the murder, and had been publicly declared as the obvious third suspect. Law enforcement had no idea about the rumors of his involvement in the death of his wife Josefina, but what if that was uncovered too?

It made no difference. Diane stuck to her story about the two intruders until the end, and she left Bill two very fond — but not loving — suicide notes.

Diane's children thought Colombany was responsible for Cecil's murder and Diane's suicide, but the suicide was never in question, and the police and FBI files show he was never seriously considered as Cecil's killer.

But where did Colombany go after he was released from prison? He never returned to Alaska, but he continued making trips to South America, including Guatemala, and was listed as a resident in Las Vegas in 1960, where he then spent the rest of his life.

It was close to publication time when I interviewed Judy Morris, and she told me that she had seen Colombany in recent years. On a trip to Las Vegas with her husband and another friend, they made a near-spontaneous decision to stop in Henderson, Nevada, where Colombany's home address was listed. His house was at the end of a cul-de-sac, and Judy recalled that it was clear he did not want to see them:

"We certainly were not welcome at that door. He got rid of us real quick."

As her friend tried to ask a question or two, Judy, who was a seamstress and worked at the famous Adrian's haberdashery in Beverly Hills as a young woman, noted that he was of a medium build, and was a "nice looking guy... the slacks he was wearing were very expensive."

Their impromptu visit had been unrevealing otherwise, but it is true to say that, like Alaska, Sin City is famously a place where people go to start over, and maybe the McAfees helped set up Colombany with a job at a casino?

As for the public records, they only show that in early 2011, Colombany was very ill. He had developed dysphagia and needed immediate gastronomy tube placement, something that required the consent of a family member or guardian. With none available that duty was taken on by Fred Nassiri, who was described as a friend of 30 years.

According to an interview with a Catholic website, Nassiri came to America from Iran in 1962 aged 20, which would seem to indicate he had first met Colombany when he was around 39 and Colombany around 56, though other sources listed Nassiri's birth date as a decade earlier. Nassiri stated in the guardianship process that he believed Colombany had no other living relatives — which was incorrect — while he himself appeared to have three children.

Nassiri's career was in wholesale fashion and real estate, and the website interview mentioned that he had been searching for meaning in life since the 1980s, and at one stage converted from Islam to Catholicism. In the early 2000s he was living an exciting life, meeting politicians including Nelson Mandela, Barack Obama, Bill Clinton and others, mostly in relation to his role as a billionaire businessman-turned-philanthropist and his 2007 song "Love Sees No Color."

An uplifting and positive 11-minute song that Nassiri wrote and performed, it had an enormously expensive video that was "filmed in 18 countries, with a cast of thousands, and sung in 15 languages with 18 directors and producers, and compiled from over 800 hours of footage," and featured Nassiri dressed in white and surrounded by children.

But in 2011, his priority had been getting the treatment his gravely-ill friend needed. Unfortunately, William Colombany died just a few days later, aged 87, the death certificate listing his occupation as iron worker and giving the cause of death as end-stage debility and rhabdomyolysis, with dementia a significant condition too. There was no autopsy or police report that I could find, and he was cremated at the Eastern Palm Mortuary.

Colombany's will was only a page long, and it was signed and dated November 1991. It listed Nassiri as executor and sole beneficiary, with the documents again noting that the Petitioner, Nassiri, believed that Colombany had no surviving family (Colombany's mother Rebecca had died in 1988), and that he never married and had no children. However, Colombany had been briefly married to Florence Rae Bailey, and there was "Josefina" in El Salvador before that too.

Colombany's assets included a bank account of close to $300,000, and his home in Henderson was valued at around $200,000. A hearing date was set for the probate, but by then someone else had become involved: Colombany's older sister Marina.

Not only had she engaged a lawyer, but the document listed the details of Investigation & Recovery at Nevada State Welfare, the department that, among other things, looked into welfare fraud. Had Marina learned about her brother's death and was concerned — or even suspicious — about what was happening with his estate? No further action was taken however, and Nassiri was listed as living at the Henderson address for about six years.

After finally tracking Nassiri down, he insisted that the William Colombany he knew was different to the one I was researching, and was very clear that he did not want to be involved in any way. So that latter part of Colombany's life, post-Alaska at least, will have to remain a mystery — at least here.

So, that leaves us with the last theory; the one that Danforth, Stevens, the pulp magazines and many others always had.

CHAPTER 32

The Alaskan Blonde

After looking at one of the crime scene photographs of Cecil's dead body, Glynn Martin wrote:

"Presence of watch suggests robbery not a factor, however victim's presence under covers holds numerous possibilities, such as surreptitious entry, stowaway in room or closet, gunshot through an open window or doorway, or assailant was trusted by the victim."

Those last words, "assailant was trusted by the victim," really stood out.

Glynn had mentioned the possibility of a forced entry, and that Cecil could have been shot from a distance, rather than close-up. Both of those tallied with Diane's account and Haggland's autopsy report, though Danforth told the coroner's inquest that he thought Cecil had been shot from the side of the bed she had slept on.

While the pillow underneath Cecil's head could have deadened the sound of the shot, I asked Glynn how it was possible no one heard anything at all. He straight away recalled two cases he had worked — one in a crowded bar, one in a gas station — where exactly that had happened. He added that television programs from "Adam 12" and "Dragnet" onward made it seem like crimes were always solved quickly, and so juries started to expect something similar, like someone always hearing a gunshot, even if the reality was quite different.

He added that Johnny's lawyers would certainly have mentioned the lack of any such sound in a trial.

Another photograph I sent him was of Diane with her two black eyes, and his response to this was extremely telling:

"Relationship issues are the number one factor in homicides, and given that I just saw a photo of a beaten woman, she would likely be the first stop for investigators."

It was striking how clear-minded he was about what he thought had happened, as he said had seen it "many, many times" when he was an officer on the beat.

It was the face of a woman who had been beaten by her husband.

At the time Diane denied they had quarreled or that Cecil had ever struck her, and Judy Morris said that if Diane wasn't happy in her marriage, "she never pretended to be happy." She added that Diane was "really tough," coming home from hospital just two days after giving birth to Marquam.

However, when I told Glynn that Diane said she was attacked by two masked men who broke into their apartment he simply nodded, and said that this was a common excuse women (and some men) used to explain away the bruises, either out of shame, embarrassment, or fear. Anonymous intruders were frequently blamed for murder, too.

Other residents of the Northward mentioned arguments, shouting and screaming coming from the Wells' apartment, and ex-wife Ethel testified at the inquest into Cecil's murder that he had struck her on numerous occasions, even in public. Judy had witnessed Cecil beating Ethel too, and Diane had excused a bruise on her face by telling her "Oh, that's just Cecil."

Cecil Junior described his father as an S-O-B who had a "kind of a history" of not being able to get on with his wives, but he never saw "any antagonism" between Cecil and Diane. He did however admit it was possible there was some violence, and that Diane might have "retaliated."

Judy was more definite, and was upset — but not surprised — when she had heard about Cecil's death. She immediately dismissed talk of a home invasion as a "good story," and rebuffed any other local gossip too:

"I just know that was Cecil. It was just one of those big fights, and he went in and went to bed. And she went in and shot him…".

Domestic abuse often thrives in male-dominated cultures like Fairbanks, and it often makes the likelihood of DH (Domestic Homicide) far greater. Talk of the Town murder victim Annette Mae Wood seemed — rightly —

to have feared her partner, and while the role that domestic violence might have played in Cecil's murder was never investigated, a front-page headline in the *FDNM* in September 1955 was revealing:

"Husband Dies of Pistol Wound - Mrs. Kennison hospitalized after taking savage beating."

After they had been out for dinner, Fairbanks club owner Douglas Kennison had suddenly begun beating his wife Mary Lee, and then shot himself in the head. She lost several teeth and had a fractured jaw, and her face was "almost unrecognizable." An unnamed police officer stated:

"If you thought Diane Wells was beat up, you should take a look at this woman."

I couldn't help but wonder whether Ted Stevens, who visited the Kennison crime scene, overheard that comment or read about it the next day.

Another clue about what might have led to Cecil's murder was something I initially missed in the police report. In March 1953, Diane made a call from a local ACS (Administration for Children's Services) office, and the statements people gave about crying children at the Northward does raise the possibility she had been concerned about Marquam's safety.

Cecil may have had his suspicions about Diane and Johnny, and the *Sunday News* wrote that "everybody knew he was extremely jealous and forever checking on Diana's (sic) whereabouts." Then again, he may not have known about Diane's two estranged daughters after all, or a jealous Ethel had told him something incendiary, which was what Saundra thought had ignited the fatal argument.

Also, if Cecil had found out that their marriage was illegitimate, as was their son Marquam, that would have been difficult to say the least. But since it never came up officially, we have to assume this was still a secret.

More simply, perhaps their marriage just wasn't working, and the expensive jewels and luxurious trappings of the Northward Building had become a dark and even lonely place for Diane. Darrell Rafferty noted wryly that if Cecil had been "as conscientious about his marriages as he was in business, he'd have been a winner. But he was a workaholic, and he was very unlucky, and not cut out for matrimony."

That Cecil's headstone read "He Loved Alaska Foremost" is probably entirely accurate.

Alternatively, many people thought that Diane, and maybe Johnny, had been driven to kill by the oldest motivation of all: greed. Mary Lou Halvorson echoed the thoughts of many others when she said that her parents, Reuben and Clara Tarte, "didn't trust Diane. They thought she was a gold digger." Later she added, hesitantly, that the words "racy, cheap, bimbo or card girl" could have been used to describe Diane.

Some of those words may have fallen out of fashion, but that assumption is still made about such relationships today, especially when they're between an older man and a younger woman. It's more socially acceptable for a man to romance a younger woman, but her acceptance of him is always greeted with raised eyebrows. The same judgment is rarely applied when the roles are reversed however, though both are often presumed to be about little more than vanity, money, and sex.

It was true that Cecil's death would make Diane a rich woman, at least on paper, but in reality she was soon selling off furniture while her new estate was snowed under with bills. Soon under arrest and then indictment, her access to any money would have been severely limited, and Darrell noted that "Cecil was worth quite a bit more alive than he was dead." He added that Diane would have been sorely disappointed "if she thought she could get the money and run. She didn't count on the buzzards picking up the scraps."

Though it was more of a factor in her suicide, the role that mental illness and depression played can't be ruled out in relation to Diane's long-term state of mind. Earlier in her life she had been under medical care for what Saundra called a "nervous breakdown" before and after her birth (perhaps pre- or post-natal depression), and at some stage she had been prescribed antidepressants.

Diane had reportedly been depressed and even suicidal after the murder, and she told reporters about her severe headaches too. Additionally, with several members of her children's family displaying mental health issues, and one of them also committing suicide, it could seem that it has moved down the generations.

Then there was the potentially toxic mix of guns and alcohol. On the night of the murder Cecil had at least four cocktails, and Ethel had testified (and Judy spoken later) about how he could get violent when he drank. Sarah Crawford Isto said the opposite, that Cecil "wasn't known to be a drunk," but on that night both things had been close to hand.

So if Diane did kill Cecil, then why did she do it?

CHAPTER 33

October 17, 1953

Based on my interviews and the documented — and new — evidence, I created what I consider to be the most likely reconstruction of the night of October 17, 1953.

It probably started with a petty argument that slowly got out of hand, and finally led to violence and murder.

After getting home from the movie at 11.20pm, later than they had planned, Cecil and Diane stayed up maybe another hour or so, and both had another drink before retiring. Diane went to collect Marquam, who had been babysat by his grandmother Frances a few floors below, but she explained that he'd been a handful all evening, and had only just gone off to sleep. He'd be a devil to get back to bed if they woke him now, so they'd have to just pop in and see him before they left the next morning.

Disappointed and angry, Diane returned to the apartment. Cecil was already snoring, and she gave him a good shove when she got into bed. Sometime after that, she woke up and ran to the bathroom to vomit. Cecil, woken by the noise and probably still affected by the bourbon he had been drinking, grumpily handed or threw her a spare pair of his pajamas.

"We're going to be late," he snapped, and made a crack about how Diane shouldn't have eaten "fried meat" for dinner. Diane waved away his concerns, saying that it was hours before they had to leave, and that she wouldn't have been sick if he hadn't insisted on bringing Herb Mensing around for dinner. They were supposed to have seen the early show at The Empress, but that went out the window too, which is why she hadn't had time to get packed.

They needed to leave early the next day for the opening of Anchorage

213

Airport, and Cecil mentioned once again how this was a big deal, now that he was the new chairman of the All Alaska Chamber of Commerce. He missed seeing Diane rolling her eyes at this, and lectured her that because Alaska Airlines' morning flight wouldn't get them there in time, he was going to fly them there in his Cessna — and so he needed his sleep. Also, why she wasn't packed?

Perhaps he now saw Diane rolling her eyes, and their petty row quickly escalated as they argued in frantic, hushed tones. Then it turned physical, the two of them flailing at each other as they jerked around the living room, with the red coral jewelry she was wearing getting snapped off in the struggle. Then Cecil was brutal, hitting Diane in the face. Dazed, she knocked the flowerpot off the table and dropped to the floor, falling unconscious soon after.

Angry, Cecil turned out the living room light and made his way back to bed.

When Diane came round her face felt tender, and she was groggy. She stumbled into the kitchen, unknowingly leaving blood on the pressure cooker, and tried to act like everything was normal by getting ready for the day ahead. Maybe she put on a pot of coffee, then set about packing (including the black shoes), and slowly getting dressed. Cecil was still snoring, as usual, so she turned on the living room light and tiptoed around before she went into her bathroom to wash, brush her teeth, and put on makeup.

She had noticed some dark stains on her borrowed pajamas, but then, already fearing what she might see, she looked in the mirror. Her eyes weren't feeling puffy from a lack of sleep; they were slowly swelling up, and there were flecks of dried blood on her cheek and lips.

She prided herself on her looks, and he liked the way she looked, but he hated the attention she got too, which is why she thought that at times like these, he deliberately tried to ruin them. He had been talking about this airport event for weeks, and she knew that he would want all the eyes on him, not her, when they were there. So now there was going to be no Anchorage trip for her; no playing the role of Cecil's charming and beautiful wife today. She might not be able to leave the apartment for a while either, as the best make-up couldn't cover this damage. People would stare, and they would know. They would gossip about it, maybe even revel in it.

Hurt, angry, and humiliated, Diane also knew that she couldn't go to the police. Even if they believed her, Cecil would talk away the bruises, and then she'd have to go back to the apartment with him. Thank goodness Marquam wasn't here, thought Diane: at least he didn't see us fighting.

When she came out of the bathroom, she saw a roll of dollar bills on the telephone table. It was the $1,000 that Cecil kept hidden in the table's secret compartment, and always left for her when he was going out of town. He put it there deliberately, Diane thought, because he knew what he'd done to her.

She looked in another mirror, and in that moment, she made a decision. Whether this was the first or the fiftieth occasion their rows had turned violent, she was going to make sure it was the last time. She may have just wanted to scare Cecil when she scrabbled for the gun and strode in to the darkened bedroom.

She hissed defiantly at him, but when he didn't even stir — didn't even apologize, or even when he said something nasty to her out of the darkness — she shouted, stepped forward, and opened fire.

Cecil barely seemed to move. Did he even hear what she said? She could smell that the gun had fired, and she instantly began to worry that someone must have heard the shot, yet Cecil still seemed to be asleep. Then she understood what had happened, and in horror at what she had done, she held her breath and waited for someone to start banging at the door. But no one did.

Shaking, she stumbled back into the living room and picked up the telephone to call someone that would help her, or would at least understand what she had done. An endless minute or two later, there was a quiet but hurried knocking at the door. Diane opened it slowly, and the man failed to hide his shock when he saw her face. Moving quickly into the apartment he glanced at Diane's bloodied pajamas, saw the gun on the telephone table, and disappeared into the bedroom. Moments later, he came back without saying a word.

Also having raced to the Northward in response to her call, two more people arrived. The hastily-assembled visitors shared their commiserations and suspicions about Diane and Cecil's marriage, and it wouldn't have been too hard for them to come up with a plan now that it had ended, albeit so violently and abruptly.

A pair of murderous thieves were on the loose in Fairbanks, and removing some jewelry would have been easy, as was throwing Cecil's now-empty wallet where it would be quickly found. Diane took the $1,000 too, as she knew Marquam and her were going to need it, no matter what happened. There were also muttered conversations about "getting rid of it," and when Diane looked at where she had put the gun down, it was gone.

The sun was slowly rising when she hugged and mumbled thanks to her friends, who all promised her that she would get through this: that they would all get through this together. Then, after they had checked the corridor outside, Diane was left alone.

It was silent again, and she took a couple of minutes to contain her panic.

Everything she had was at stake, maybe including her life. Prison would be the end for her and Marquam, and what chance would she ever have to see her daughters again? She knew that people thought she was a gold-digger, and if her affair with Johnny came to light, she would be condemned before she got to trial — and these bruises wouldn't have counted for anything.

She looked back at the darkened bedroom, and then began to go into shock when she realized they had made a mistake: how had the "thieves" got in to the apartment? She wouldn't have let strangers in at such an odd hour, and damaging the door locks would have been dangerously noisy, so the only option seemed to be the connecting door.

Apartment 814 was further down the dead-end corridor, so the "thieves" could conceivably have gained access there and then come through the connecting door into apartment 815. It didn't look or sound convincing, but then Diane heard the sound of the elevator, and she had to quickly improvise.

She sat for a while, listening to see if anyone else was leaving their apartment, and then through her fresh tears she shouted "it hurts, it hurts" loudly enough for the notorious vents and any neighbors to hear, then threw open the front door to raise the alarm. As she stumbled towards the apartment door opposite, she silently prayed that her friends were right.

And they were — at least until Diane decided she wanted to end her story.

Epilogue

I often cursed my luck for coming across this story at least 20 years too late, but at least I knew my answer to the question everybody has been asked at one time or another: if you could travel back in time, where would you go?

I would undoubtedly choose Fairbanks, Alaska, on the night of October 16, 1953.

Of course, the rules of time travel are that you can't — or shouldn't — change anything, because it will then alter the future, and always for the worse. I stand by my choice though, because after five years of research and interviews I am certain that if I could say exactly what happened that night, several future generations of people would be closer, happier, and, in Diane's case perhaps, may have lived a longer life.

The murder of Cecil Wells may have been decades ago, but the fact it was never solved has led to generational trauma. Among the Wells, Warren and Colombany families there are stories of orphanages, broken homes, divorce, estrangement, violence, abuse, mental illness, secrets, and suicide. With few exceptions, it seems like everyone who was touched by this case has suffered in some way.

They will never really get closure, and they deserve more than that, which was the reason I tried not to speculate too much — except for the last chapter.

However, sometimes the facts, the coincidences, and the tragedies seemed hard to believe.

There was the fact that 5-year-old-Susanna, whose mother was murdered by her lover, was adopted by Clara and Johnny Warren. Just a few weeks later, Johnny was accused of killing his lover.

Also, what were the chances that Diane's grandson committed suicide near the hotel where she had taken her fatal dose of barbiturates?

Or what about E.V. Danforth, the Chief of Police who resigned shortly

217

after the murder? He had vowed to stay in Fairbanks, but ending up joining the police in Oregon. There he filed for bankruptcy, his petition reportedly including money he had "borrowed" while serving in Fairbanks. A few weeks after Colombany was found guilty, Danforth and his wife Adelene welcomed a baby son — but the child died soon after.

There have been further murders at the Northward Building, too: a 1974 stabbing, a still-unsolved killing in 1986, a man beaten to death in his room in 2011, and most recently in August 2020, when a 59-year-old woman was last seen alive at there. She is still missing.

In 2000, in recognition of his many years serving Alaska, Anchorage Airport was renamed in honor of Ted Stevens. It must have been a strangely bittersweet moment for him, as his wife Ann and four others had died in crash at that very airport in 1978 — he and one other person survived. Tragically, Stevens died in a floatplane crash near Aleknagik, Alaska, in 2010. As in 1978, there were five victims, while four survived.

Following the *Compiled Laws of the Territory of Alaska* (1949), Stevens indicted Diane and Johnny for first-degree murder, a charge that, in part, is defined as involving "deliberate and premeditated malice."

But I don't think Diane planned to murder Cecil, nor do I think she lay in wait for him.

Today, some might argue that with the apparent complications of Cecil and Diane's marriage, her medical and psychological history, and arguably the circumstantial evidence against her, that she warranted a second-degree murder charge, which instead included the terms "purposely and maliciously." Then there is manslaughter (defendant "unlawfully kills another"), and though all are rather closely related, other issues might have come into play during a trial.

The sentences for these offenses varied as well. First-degree murder had the penalty of death (or as would have been more likely in her case, life in prison with hard labor), while the others are "not less than fifteen years" imprisonment, and between one to twenty years respectively.

Ironically, Diane's glamorous looks, which seemed to turn the press and public against her during the investigation, might actually have been very helpful if she had gone to trial.

From Greek tales to Biblical stories and right up to the live-tweeted media circus trials of today, women have long escaped punishment thanks to their physical beauty. Despite their best efforts to be objective, jury members of both sexes will often vote for acquittal no matter what the circumstances, and all lawyers will (at least privately) consider beauty as a key defense strategy.

They will insist their client was the abused victim rather than a cold-blooded killer, and while it might be as cynical as crocodile tears, over and over again it's been shown that if she's considered pretty enough, a woman can literally get away with murder.

There was no trial for Diane though, and just the fact that she allegedly conspired with an African-American lover would likely have been her downfall, as their sexual relationship would have shocked and offended too many at that time.

Additionally, even though she wrote it under the influence of barbiturates, the "I am guilty..." suicide note seemed like a confession, and many saw it that way. She clearly felt guilty about what happened to Cecil, even if she wasn't the person who fired a .380 bullet into his head.

A few weeks after her suicide, the infamous Country Club photograph of Diane, Cecil and Johnny, the image that more or less condemned her in the public eye, was splashed across the front page of the *Los Angeles Herald-Express*. Further down that same page, there's a small article reporting that a man had committed suicide at a well-known hotel in Los Angeles.

It was the Hollywood Plaza Hotel.

Bibliography

Bagoy, John P. *Legends and Legacies: Anchorage 1910 - 1935, Remembering Our Buried Past*: Publication Consultants, 2001

Best, C.H./Taylor, N.B. *The Physiological Basis of Medical Practice* –Williams & Wilkins: Baltimore, 1990

Brown, Tricia/Corral, Roy. *Fairbanks: Alaska's Heart of Gold* –Alaska Northwest Books: Portland, 2000

Cole, Dermot. *Fairbanks: A Gold Rush Town That Beat The Odds* –Epicenter Press: Kenmore, 1999

Cole, Dermot. *Frank Barr: Bush Pilot in Alaska and the Yukon* –Alaska Northwest Publishing Company: Edmonds, 1986

Cole, Terrence. *Fighting for the Forty-Ninth Star: C.W. Snedden and the Crusade for Alaska Statehood* –University of Alaska Foundation: Fairbanks, 2010

Cole, Terrence. *E.T. Barnette: The Strange Story of the Man Who Founded Fairbanks* –Northwest Publishing Company: Anchorage, 1981

Crawford Isto, Sarah. *Good Company: A Mining Family in Fairbanks, Alaska* –University of Alaska Press: Fairbanks, 2007

Faulconer, Tom. *In the Eyes of the Law: The True Story of Love, Betrayal, Murder, Fame and Justice in 1950's America* –1st Books: 2002

Ferber, Edna. *Ice Palace* –Doubleday & Company, Inc: New York, 1958

Gardner, Erle S. *The Court of Last Resort* –W. Sloane Associates: New York, 1952

Gibran, Khalil. *The Prophet* –Alfred A. Knopf: New York, 1986

Hancock, Robert. *Ruth Ellis: The Last Woman To Be Hanged* –Weidenfeld and Nicolson: London, 1963

Heaton, John W. *Outlaw Tales of Alaska: True Stories of the Last Frontier's Most Infamous Crooks, Culprits, and Cutthroats* –Two Dot: Guilford, 2010

Hunt, William R. *Distant Justice: Policing the Alaskan Frontier* –University of Oklahoma Press: Norman, 1987

James, Laura. *The Beauty Defense: Femme Fatales on Trial* –Kent State University Press: Kent, 2020

Keve, Paul W. *The McNeil Century: The Life and Times of an Island Prison* –Nelson-Hall: Chicago, 1984

Kynell, K.S. *A Different Frontier: Alaska Criminal Justice, 1935-1965* –University Press of America: Maryland, 1991

McClowsky, William B. *Highliners* –Lyons & Burford: Guilford, 1995

Morgan, Lael. *Good Time Girls of the Alaska-Yukon Gold Rush* –Epicenter Press: Kenmore, 2009

Naske, Claus M./Rowinski, Ludwig J. *Fairbanks: A Pictorial History* –The Donning Company: Virginia Beach, 1995

Rennick, Penny (editor) *Fairbanks: Volume 22, Number 1* –Alaska Geographic: Anchorage, 1995

Snyder, LeMoyne. *Homicide Investigation: A Book of Practical Information for Coroners, Police Officers and other Investigators* –Charles C. Thomas: Springfield, 1944

Reynolds, Ruth. "The Playgirl And the Drummer" –*Sunday News*, Volume 36, No. 13, July 29, 1956, p16-17

Fullon, Richard T. "Death and the Midas Touch" –*Front Page Detective*, Vol 14, No. 9, February 1954, p21-23, 69-70

Heise, Jack. "The Millionaire, the Fifth Wife, and the Drummer Boy" – *Official Detective Stories*, Vol. XXIII, No. 1, p8-11, 49-50

"Drummer and Blonde" –*Newsweek*, Vol XLII, No.20, November 16, 1953, p38-39

"The Case Of The Beat-Up Blonde" –*Life*, Vol 35, No. 22, November 30, 1953, p52-54

"The Blonde Beauty & The Black Drummer" –*The Truth*, No. 2818, March 21, 1954, p19 (Australia)

"Murder trial wife on bail" –*Daily Herald*, No. 11750, Nov 11, 1953, p2 (United Kingdom)

"Blonde, Drummer Held In Millionaire's Murder" –*Jet*, Vol. V, No. 2, Nov 19, 1953, p14

"New Suspect In Murder Crime May Clear Drummer" –*Jet*, Vol. V. No. 5, Dec 10, 1953, p29

"Police Chief Quits In Alaska Murder Case" –*Jet*, Vol. V, No. 6 Dec 17, 1953, p6

"Blonde Beauty Kills Herself" –*Jet*, Vol. V, No. 20, March 25, 1954, p26

The Compiled Laws of the Territory of Alaska 1913 –Document 1093, Washington Government Printing Office: Washington, D.C., 1913

The Compiled Laws of the Territory of Alaska 1949 –Volumes I and III, Bancroft Whitney: San Francisco, 1948

United States Census 1950 –Volume II, Part 51, Chapter C, United States Government Printing Office: Washington D.C., 1952

Uniform Crime Reporting Program Annual Report –*Crime in Alaska 2019*, Criminal Records & Identification Bureau: Anchorage, 2020

Homicide in the United States 1950-1964 –Series 20, Number 6, National Center for Health Statistics: Washington, D.C., 1967

Kefauver Final Committee Report: Organized Crime In Interstate Commerce – No 278, United States Government Printing Office: Washington, D.C., 1951

Winstanley, E.A. *Annual Report Coroner Los Angeles County California July 1, 1953 –June 30, 1954*: Los Angeles, 1954

Keve, Paul W. "The Bop's Alaskan Adventure" –*Federal Prisons Journal*, Vol 2, No 4: US Department of Justice, 1992, p43-46, p55

Robertson Blackmore, Emma et al. "Previous prenatal loss as a predictor of perinatal depression and anxiety" –*British Journal of Psychiatry*, May 2011

Claus Naske interviews Judge Everett W. Hepp. Oral History No. 82-68-07 – Alaska Court System History Tapes: Washington, July 30/31, 1982

Charles Fedullo interviews Michael Carey about Senator Ted Stevens. Ted Stevens Papers Project, Oral History 2009-13-02 –University of Alaska Fairbanks: Anchorage, May 26, 2009

www.ancestry.com

www.newspapers.com

https://www.waltdisney.org/blog/walt-and-sharon-take-trip-alaska

https://www.abortionrecovery.ca

https://www.mayoclinic.org

www.apa.org

www.medicalnewstoday.com

www.nassiri.com

https://www.onlinenevada.org/articles/guy-mcafee

https://obscureactresses.wordpress.com/2015/04/23/june-brewster/

http://publichistorypdx.org/2017/03/12/big-jim-elkins-gangsters-unions-pinball/

https://daily.jstor.org/alaskas-unique-civil-rights-struggle/

www.deathpenaltyinfo.org

https://worldpopulationreview.com/state-rankings/crime-rate-by-state

www.timetableimages.com

https://vilda.alaska.edu/

https://www.filmpreservation.org

https://live.laborstats.alaska.gov/cen/hist.html

https://trove.nla.gov.au/

https://www.notoriousbarsofak.com

United States vs. Cecil Wells and Maud Raudabaugh –Case No. 1943, 1946-B (1928)

William E. Aspee vs. Diane Walker Aspee –No. 415382, Vol. 1383, p869 (1950)

Florence R. Colombany vs. William B. Colombany –No. A-8919, Journal g31, p88 (1953)

Inquest of the Body of Cecil M. Wells (Deceased) –Case No. 285 (1953)

United States of America vs. Johnny Warren and Diane Wells –Case No. 1770 (1953-1960)

In the Matter of Estate of Annette Wood (Deceased) –No. 1633 (1953-1956)

Federal Bureau of Investigation: Cecil Moore Wells (Deceased), Diane Wells, Victim –File No: 95-1424 (1953-1960)

Los Angeles Police Department, Report No. 399195 – May, Doris (Suicide) (1954)

Office of County Coroner, Los Angeles –Case No. 93284 –Diana Wells (1954)

In the Matter of the Estate of Diane Wells, Deceased –Case No. 1700 (1954-1967)

United States of America vs. William Colombany –Case No. 1994 cr (1955)

Petition for Appointment of Temporary and Permanent Guardian of the Person and Estate of William Colombany –Case No. G-11-035031-A (2011)

In the Matter of the Estate of William B. Colombany (Deceased) –Case No. P-11-070525-E (2011)

Fairbanks Daily News-Miner
Anchorage Times
Anchorage Daily News
Daily Sitka Sentinel
Alaska Weekly
Jessen's Weekly (Fairbanks)

Los Angeles Times
Los Angeles Examiner
Los Angeles Herald-Express
Los Angeles Daily News
Los Angeles Mirror
Oakland Tribune
San Francisco Chronicle
San Francisco Call-Bulletin
San Bernardino Sun (California)
Auburn Journal (California)

Seattle Times
Seattle Post-Intelligencer
Morning Oregonian
Pittsburgh Courier
Indianapolis Recorder
Stars and Stripes

About The Author

Originally from London, James T. Bartlett has been living in Los Angeles since 2004.

As a travel and lifestyle journalist and historian, he has written for the *Los Angeles Times*, BBC, *Los Angeles Magazine, ALTA California, High Life, Hemispheres, Westways, American Way*, Atlas Obscura, *The Guardian, Daily Mirror, Real Crime, Ripperologist Magazine, History Ireland, Bizarre* and *Variety*, among others.

In 2012 he published *Gourmet Ghosts – Los Angeles*, an alternative guide to the history and ghost stories behind some of the city's oldest bars, restaurants and hotels, while 2016's *Gourmet Ghosts 2* focused on true crimes that took place at more of L.A.'s notable locations and eateries.

The books led to lectures, events, book club hosting, and appearances on radio, podcasts, and television shows including *Ghost Adventures* and *The UnXplained*. You can find out more information at www.gourmetghosts.com and @gourmetghosts / #gourmetghosts

Much more information, pictures and documents about *The Alaskan Blonde* and the murder of Cecil Wells can be found at www.thealaskanblonde.com and on Instagram and Facebook @thealaskanblonde

Made in the USA
Middletown, DE
28 May 2022